Beyond Stereotypes

Bilingual Press/Editorial Bilingüe

Studies in the Language and Literature
of United States Hispanos

Address
Bilingual Press
Box M, Campus Post Office
SUNY-Binghamton
Binghamton, New York 13901
(607) 724-9495

Beyond Stereotypes

The Critical Analysis of Chicana Literature

edited by

María Herrera-Sobek

Bilingual Press/Editorial Bilingüe
BINGHAMTON, NEW YORK

ISBN: 0-916950-54-9
Printed simultaneously in a softcover edition. ISBN: 0-916950-55-7

Library of Congress Catalog Card Number: 84-73316

PRINTED IN THE UNITED STATES OF AMERICA

Cover design by Christopher J. Bidlack

Table of Contents

Acknowledgments

This important collection of articles would not have been possible without the moral and financial support of various agencies and individuals. I want to express my most sincere appreciation to the following groups and persons who saw the significance of this project and contributed to its success: Chancellor Daniel G. Aldrich, Jr., and the Chancellor's Club Fund; Vice Chancellor William J. Lillyman and the Ethnic Studies Fund; Vice Chancellor John Whiteley, Dean of Students; Dean of Humanities Kendall Bailes; Carla Espinoza and the Affirmative Action Office; the Women's Program Board; the Chicano-Latino Colloquium; La Raza Association; the Spanish and Portuguese Department; and Dr. Rita Peterson, Director of the Education Department. My thanks also to Tony Luna, Sylvia and Howard Lenhoff, Fred Flores, Rudolfo and Pat Anaya, Jeanne and Roy Giodano, Helen Johnson, Educational Testing Service, Alejandro Morales, Jaime Rodríguez, Eloy Rodríguez, Héctor Orjuela, Julian Palley, Helen Viramontes, and of course the panelists: Helia Sheldon, the late Tomás Rivera, Sylvia Lizárraga, Francisco Lomelí, Margarita Nieto, Carlos Cortés (whose symposium paper "Chicanas in Film: History of an Image" has just appeared in *Chicano Cinema: Research, Reviews, and Resources*, published by Bilingual Review/Press), Eliud Martínez, Marta E. Sánchez, Rosaura Sánchez, Ramón Curiel, Magdalena Mora, Tey Diana Rebolledo, and past Chicano Literary Prize winners Rosemary Cadena, Helen Viramontes, Rita Mendoza, Lorenza Schmidt, Rita María Canales, Rosa Carrillo, and Rosaura Sánchez.

My sincere thanks also to Spanish Department chairs Seymour Menton and Dayle Seidenspinner Núñez and to graduate students Ivonne Gordon-Kostas, Elsa Saucedo, Noé Chávez, William Hernández, and Elizabeth Baez.

Finally, I would also like to express my gratitude to Donna Brenneis, Chicano Literary Contest coordinator, 1981-82, for helping me to organize the symposium. Finally, my heartfelt thanks to Celia Bernal, Spanish Department secretary, and Geneva López, Chicano Literary Contest coordinator, 1980-81. My special thanks to Geneva for typing parts of this manuscript.

To my Chicana sisters:
Rosa, Alicia, and Yolanda

INTRODUCTION

María Herrera-Sobek

This provocative collection of articles on Chicana writers and their works is the result of the symposium "New Perspectives in Literature: Chicana Novelists and Poets" held at the University of California at Irvine, May 4, 1982, in conjunction with the Eighth Chicano Literary Contest Award Ceremonies.

Chicana writers have always been an integral part of each year's contest and winners; it was deemed appropriate, therefore, to recognize the efforts and success of many of these authors by dedicating a symposium specifically to Chicanas in literature. The reception of the theme and structure of the proposed symposium was outstanding; scholars throughout California were extremely pleased to participate in this first conference focusing exclusively on Chicana authors.

The success and great interest generated by the symposium leads me to believe the time is past overdue for a collection of critical studies such as this that seriously examines Chicana literary creations. The articles included in this volume, therefore, are intended to be a first step in meeting this need. The series of studies presented here were originally presented at the Symposium in much shorter versions; they were subsequently expanded to article-length form for this collection.

This volume is divided into two sections. Section I encompasses those articles analyzing novels and short stories and Section II critically examines Chicana poetry.

Section I: Prose

Our lead article by Francisco Lomelí, "Chicana Novelists in the Process of Creating Fictive Voices," affords us an excellent introduction to the historical antecedents and the present emergence of Chicana prose writers. Lomelí adheres to the thesis that Chicana authors have suffered undue hardships in the area of publication due to their status as a marginal group within a marginal group. This literary critic underscores the fact that Chicanas inhabit the unenviable position of being "twice a minority." (Eliana Rivero and Margarita B. Melville had previously posited this view.) Thus, if we acknowledge these sociohistorical and political vectors impacting on the literary production of Chicana writers, it is surprising that Chicanas are "breaking out of the silence," as Rita Sánchez puts it, and are indeed engaged in productive, high-quality literary creations.

The past ten years have witnessed a very modest but nevertheless encouraging number of works of fiction by Chicanas. Berta Ornelas' *Come Down From the Mound* (1975), Isabella Ríos' *Victuum* (1976), Gina Valdés' *María Portillo* (1981), and Estela Portillo Trambley's *Trini* (forthcoming) are four examples. All of these works are critically commented upon in Lomelí's article and their contribution within Chicano letters is evaluated.

Lomelí agrees with feminist scholars such as Kate Millett and Patricia Meyer Sparks that the cultural constraints imposed on women writers strait-jacket them and prevent them from exercising a more dynamic and extensive publishing record. If women's issues and concerns are not taken seriously by a male-dominated society, then works with a female perspective will not be published; and if indeed these works get published, critics (who are generally male) will ignore or lightly pass over these works.

Lomelí further points to the contributions made by these pioneer Mexican-American women writers: Chicanas have expanded the Chicano literary space by demythifying the external image imposed upon them. These women authors have gone beyond the limiting space of virgins and prostitutes inherited from Western civilization's conceptualization of women and further utilized by Chicano authors. Chicanas, through their fictive works, have refused to be bracketed into the stereotypical roles of the past and seek instead, as Alma Villanueva so elegantly phrases it, to be "their own source of inspiration." Thus, the subject matter in *Victuum* by Isabella Ríos is giving birth and life to the protagonist; the life-experience process is traced from the moment of conception to intrauterine life and on to adulthood. Lomelí emphatically states that in both *Come Down From the Mound* and in *Victuum* we find innovative approaches to depicting aspects that pertain to humanity's concern with the life-experience process and further adds that by so doing Chicana novelists "offer new perspectives and nuances to Chicano expression." Lomelí's article orients us to the historical and literary context in which Chicana authors find themselves.

Carmen Salazar Parr and Genevieve M. Ramírez, on the other hand, posit in their article "The Female Hero in Chicano Literature" a startling and innovative reconceptualization of the term "hero" vis-à-vis women protagonists. Salazar Parr and Ramírez seek to discard the confining stereotypical term "heroine" which generally serves as backdrop for the engaging actions of the male protagonist. Instead of seeing female protagonists as heroines, they redefine the term "hero" in order to encompass both female and male protagonists within its meaning. By liberating the term from its limited confines they proceed to apply Joseph Campbell's paradigm of the hero adventure to various Chicana novels, short stories, and plays. Through this reconceptualization of the term "hero" we indeed see what previously might have been called "heroines" follow the pattern of the nuclear monomyth posited by Campbell, which he in turn based on the structure of the *rites de passage:* Separation, Initiation, and Return. Having established this connection, Salazar Parr and Ramírez proceed to the analysis of Josefina Niggli's plays *Soldadera* (1936) and *The Ring of General Macías* (1943); Estela Portillo Trambley's short story "The Trees" (from *Rain of Scorpions,* 1975) and her novel *Trini* (forthcoming); and Gina Valdés' *María Portillo* (1981). In all these works, the images of strong resilient women are most evident; Niggli's works once again debunk the stereotypical view of the passive, submissive Chicana/Mexicana.

Rosaura Sánchez' provocative article "Chicana Prose Writers: The Case of Gina Valdés and Sylvia Lizárraga" takes the position that Chicana writers "can only be studied as a separate segment of literature if sex in itself determines a particular mode of writing, perspective or content." "In the case of Chicana writers," she further states, "perspective and content have differed only to the degree that the literary work has focused on women, their sexuality, their oppression and their creative power." Actually, what distinguishes Chicana writers from their male counterparts is "their relative invisibility." Thus, the significant factor in Chicana versus Chicano literary productivity rests, according to R. Sánchez, squarely on the shoulders of Chicano literary critics, professors, and publishers. The male control of Chicano publication enterprises is a most important element in the analysis of Chicana literary production.

Rosaura Sánchez presents a compelling case for the reexamination of Chicano *machismo* and shortsighted discriminatory practices visited upon Chicanas by members of their own group.

It is imperative that as a people concerned with the racism of the Anglo establishment, we look into our own forms of sexism that short-circuit and stifle the creativity and literary genius of half of our population. The charge of mediocrity or inferior artistic creation cannot be utilized to substantiate discriminatory practices because the evidence points to the contrary. Works by Chicana writers are equal or superior in merit, aesthetics, and creative composition to those of Chicanos, particularly in poetry, where artistic expression has surpassed most of them. R. Sánchez further points to the beginning of a vigorous spiritual tradition in Chicana prose writings as exemplified by such authors as Sylvia Lizárraga and Gina Valdés.

Eliud Martínez, in his article, "Personal Vision in the Short Stories of Estela Portillo Trambley," further substantiates (although unintentionally) Rosaura Sánchez' point. In this analysis, Martínez explores the artistic construction of Estela Portillo Trambley's short stories in her collection *Rain of Scorpions* (1975) and finds that her works are characterized by an elegant style of writing, a love of life, and a deep philosophical/mystical sense toward humanity and the universe. Portillo Trambley exemplifies another vision of Chicano expression: the elegantly crafted, cultured, and widely read Chicana author. This is not to say that she is not a thoroughly engagée or committed author. On the contrary, this Mexican-American author masterfully weaves a social protest commentary with elegance of thought and aesthetic expression. Martínez points out the wide literary influences seen in Portillo Trambley: Bergson, Jung, Jaspers, Nietzsche, Huxley, the Bible, Toynbee, Aisley, Buddha, Lao-Tzu, Kahlil Gibran, Pierre Teilhard de Chardin, T. S. Eliot, Proust, Sartre, Genet, the Russian novelists, and Mexican and Latin American thinkers and writers. The author herself in an interview granted to Bruce Novoa (published in *Chicano Authors: Inquiry by Interview,* 1980) has acknowledged her literary antecedents and her thirst for knowledge and "life." Martínez posits that Portillo Trambley's personal vision emanates from a combination of language and style. He sees this particular writer as one who "venerates" language, who delights in and savors both the beauty and power of the world. Thus, Martínez concludes that her language is eloquent, exquisite, correct; her style philosophical, erudite, conceptual.

One has to agree that Portillo Trambley evokes a mythic vision of the universe and intuits an intense relationship between humankind and the cosmos. Within her stories underlie the structures of time, honor, myths, and Garden of Eden, the myth of Dionysus, the Quest, man as pilgrim, and the sacrifice, to name a few. Her social protest is manifested in a feminist posture which she has acknowledged b which had not been "intentionally" devised. Estela Portillo Trambley's female protagonists fight back against an oppressive system that stifles feminine creativity and free will. Her women are more often than not victorious in their relentless opposition to a *machista,* repressive system and thus can serve as role models for other Chicanas wishing to strike out and melt the chains of thought and custom that enslave them and relegate them to a third-class citizenship.

Section II: Poetry

In beauty, craftsmanship, and originality Chicana poets are outstanding indeed. They compare most favorably with Chicano poets and perhaps even surpass them. In the poetic, lyrical genre Chicanas have found their space and inhabit it with confidence and pride. Tey Diana Rebolledo examines a little known facet of Chicana creativity and genius: humor. Rebolledo's article proceeds from the position that humor on women in general has not received the attention it deserves. "Women's humor as a *social process,*" she posits, "has not been studied analytically." And of course, in general, scholars have ignored women's humor.

Rebolledo, in her article "Walking the Thin Line: Humor in Chicana Literature," seeks to explore the reasons for this neglect on the part of scholars, and—since wit is not absent in Chicana writers—her article presents an incisive analysis of this phenomenon in the poetry (and some prose) of Chicanas. Rebolledo's contribution lies in pinpointing the varities of humor present in the works of Chicana authors and most importantly in delineating the relationship between humor and sexist oppression which underscores this particular humor.

Anthropologists as well as depth psychologists assert that joke telling is an aggressive act. Latent feelings of hostility, anxiety, and repression often manifest themselves through jokes. Rebolledo indeed discovers that Chicana wit is invariably hostile to males and more significantly that due to this hostility, Chicana humor veers precariously between laughter and crying.

Through humor, once again, we find the Chicana writer attempting to break the constricting cultural stereotypes she has for so long borne. Thus we encounter both the sparks of rebellion through the clever manipulation of language and those dark moments of self-parody and self-disparagement. Caught between two strong cultural currents, American and Mexican, and feeling the pressures to conform and acculturate on one side and to preserve and transmit the culture on the other, Chicana writers have found through their creative energies a vehicle through which feelings of anxiety and ambiguity can be expressed.

Marta Sánchez' seminal article, "The Birthing of the Poetic 'I' in Alma Villanueva's *Mother, May I?*: The Search for a Feminine Identity," combines stylistic, linguistic, psychological, and reader's response methodological approaches to render an incisive analysis of Villanueva's poetry. Her study is divided into two parts: The first part is a "close reading of a poem as a verbal artifact, or a string of words that reverberate and echo one another"; the second part examines Villanueva's poems as a "repository of meaning from which we extract a message; the poem at this level represents events and actions that explain the coming into being of the protagonist as a poet." The main thrust of Marta Sánchez' exploration into Villa-nueva's poetry is to elucidate the two principal identities, Woman or Chicana, and their ramifications, interconnections, and incorpo-ration into the poetic "I" of the character/narrator.

According to Sánchez, the book-length poem *Mother, May I?* is an excursion into the life, both spiritual and physical, of the author. Part I of *Mother, May I?* provides a glimpse into the early years: growing up Chicana in San Francisco, the series of foster homes the child bounces in and out of, and most significantly the death of the grand-mother — Villanueva's most important mentor. Part II presents the traumatic adolescent years, her marriage, pregnancy, and the experi-ence of her own birth as a poet. Part III, on the other hand, becomes more metaphoric and concentates on (1) the creative process, (2) the reproductive cycle of coitus, pregnancy, and birth, (3) the psycho-logical development of becoming a person, and (4) the artistic process of producing a "cultural artifact — a poem." Marta Sánchez believes that Villanueva's main thematic thrust is a search for her feminine identity. That is to say, the poetic consciousness present in her works does not focus on a search for identity as a Chicana but zeroes in on her identity as a woman. There exists in Villanueva's poems a concern for the central oppositions of race and sex and the confrontational dyad of a Chicano/Anglo world. However, Sánchez posits that while Villanueva is aware of her Chicano heritage and the cultural clashes and conflicts this heritage entails, she nevertheless is primarily concerned with her status as a woman.

As is evident from the above overview of the articles, there is an explicit concern by the various scholars represented in this volume with the image, status, and stereotypes of the Chicana that are promulgated in literary representations. The first part of our title, *Beyond Stereotypes*, derives from this concern. The importance granted to gender in our society and the status acquired solely on the basis of gender force Chicanas into an inferior position. Simone de Beauvoir, in her excellent historical analysis of the oppression of women *The Second Sex* (1949), delineates the social forces that converged to place women in a secondary position vis-à-vis men. Woman is defined in relation to man; the male is the norm and all else is the Other. Being a woman, the Chicana can be subsumed under the male-dominated historical perspective of other oppressed and victimized females in Western civilization and indeed throughout world history. The cultural vectors — Spanish, Indian, and Mexican — that impact on the social status of the Chicana further relegate her to a position of inferiority.

However, if history books, articles, oral tradition, and literary works portray the Chicana and her female ancestors in one particular mode, a closer examination of reality tends to disprove much that has been articulated or written about Chicanas/Mexicanas. From the very beginnings of the settlement and colonization of the American continent, both Spanish and Indian women took an active part in the success (and failure) of various expeditions and enterprises. In Nancy O'Sullivan-Beare's book *Las mujeres de los conquistadores. La mujer española en los comienzos de la colonización americana. Aportaciones para el estudio de la transculturación* (Madrid: Compañía Bibliográfica Española, 1956), for example, the author discusses the important but often-forgotten role Spanish women played in the forging of a new continent. Included in her study are fearless women governors and landed heiresses who upon the death of husbands or kin inherited and successfully managed *latifundias* and *haciendas*. The women who came to a generally undeveloped continent were no limp-wristed *señoritas* but hardy pioneers who have been forgotten and stereotyped as frivolous, fainting-prone, weak biddies hiding behind lacy mantillas.

However, logic dictates that no faint-hearted person, either male or female, could withstand the arduous rigors of crossing the ocean in sixteenth-century sailing ships lacking any semblance of comfortable quarters. Not only was the sailing of a vast and oftentimes inhospitable and "uncooperative" ocean a real test of character, but once having arrived in this land called "New Spain" there was no guarantee that the discomforts and travails suffered in a three-month journey were over. Indeed, the adventure was just beginning. Thus it stands to reason that any woman who was brave and enterprising enough to make the initial decision to emigrate from Spain and leave the comforts of European civilization far behind had to be of a strong and aggressive disposition; and make no mistake, their mettle was to be tested again and again in the New World.

Because of the relative scarcity of Spanish women, many of them contracted matrimony upon arrival or found a husband of comfortable means soon thereafter. This, of course, did not mean that the *señoras* were to lead a life of ease and luxury but, on the contrary, these women were expected to actively participate in the business of caring for and sustaining an hacienda in proper condition, a task which given the tenor of the times was no small feat. Alfredo Mirandé and Evangelina Enríquez in *La Chicana: The Mexican-American Woman* (1979) insist that:

> The frontier conditions in the borderlands made the maintenance of traditional Spanish institutions and customs difficult. Especially difficult to enforce was the concept that the women should occupy a subordinate and protected status. Adherence to a rigid sexual division of labor, in which the man was responsible for economic production and the woman for bearing and rearing children, was a luxury that could not be maintained in a subsistence economy. Women were actively involved in activities outside the home such as tending grazing herds and butchering and skinning animals, as well as planting, irrigation, and harvesting crops.[1]

In addition to the hardships involved in living in a relatively wild and virgin territory, the conquistador tended to possess an adventure-seeking type of personality and was not content to settle in his newly acquired domains. The determination of these early settlers to press on, to search for new and undiscovered empires, is now legendary. What is not legendary is the fact that many of these men took their spouses, their daughters, or other female relatives on these mind-boggling expeditions, which frequently meant trekking through thousands of miles of unexplored, oftentimes, unfriendly lands.

Modern-day Chicanas can trace their ancestors to these hardy women who accompanied their husbands in their explorations of new worlds. One such outstanding pioneer who has left her mark in historical records is María Feliciana Arballo y Gutiérrez, widow of a soldier who was to accompany Capitán de Anza's second expedition into what is now known as the U.S. Southwest. Susanna Bryant Dakin, in her study *Rose, or Rose Thorn? Three Women of Spanish California* (1963), explores the historical role of these early pioneers. She recounts the furor caused by María Feliciana's decision to form part of the De Anza expedition with her two young daughters even after her soldier husband had died.

Undaunted, the young widow placed Eustaquia on the saddle in front of her, Tomasa behind; and answered roll call. . . . She astonished the crowd of colonists and onlookers including her own close relatives, by announting that she would take her husband's place—play father and mother to their little girls—carry out the orders of the King, where it lay within her power, on the 1,600-mile ride to Spain's northernmost frontier; and afterwards in the colony to be founded on the shore of San Francisco Bay.[2]

Other eighteenth-century pioneer women such as Doña Eulalia Fages, wife of Don Pedro Fages, governor of California, and Dona Concepción Arguello, California's first nun, have managed to imprint their personalities on the pages of history and leave an important record of their contributions in the colonization and settlement of the Far West. The involvement of these women in the taming of New Spain's northernmost colonies, however, was the rule rather than the exception for each expedition generally included within its ranks wives, daughters, female servants, and sundry female kin. The contributions of these early pioneer women have laid dormant in the pages of history (when not omitted altogether) and it is only recently, stimulated by the revisionist impetus of the Women's Movement and the Chicano Movement, that we have begun to accord them the proper historical respect and acknowledge women's role in the founding of the United States' colonies. Stereotypes are hard to exterminate once they have taken root and hardened in people's minds. And so it will take a long time to eradicate stereotypical images of women that in no way conform to reality.

Not only was the role of Spanish women an active and productive one, as we have outlined above, but in a similar vein Indian women contributed in no small measure to the colonization and development of the New World. Unfortunately, this active participation has come down to future generations (including the present) as an albatross. Of course, when one speaks of the Conquest the image of a victorious Hernán Cortés looms larger-than-life in our imagination; second only to the importance of Cortés in the vanquishing of the Aztecs (in fact, sometimes even dwarfing Cortés' accomplishments) is the figure of the much maligned Doña Marina, "La Malinche," the woman who has been damned in the pages of history for having participated on the side of Cortés in the conquest of the Aztec Empire. Again the stereotype of the fallen women, the whore who sells her people to the enemy, has formed part and parcel of literary creations both in Mexico and the United States.

Recently, a reevaluation of Doña Marina has been undertaken by some Chicana scholars. Adelaida R. Del Castillo, in her article "Malintzín Tenépal: A Preliminary Look into a New Perspective" which appears in *Essays on la mujer* (1977), explores the negative image of La Malinche and offers a new interpretation of the role Doña Marina played in the Conquest. Doña Marina, in this study, is viewed as a woman betrayed by her people and not as the betrayer. She is presented as an intelligent, articulate diplomat who sought to be an intermediary between the two clashing, antagonistic forces; a woman who wanted to promote mutual understanding between the two cultures that were about to confront each other in a terrible war. Doña Marina, an early convert to Christianity, was a visionary whose only desire was to end the carnage that characterized Aztec religion toward the end of the Aztec Empire. Del Castillo presents a Doña Marina who wanted to bring to fruition the prophecies of Quetzalcóatl; in sum, a woman who was a religious activist working on "behalf of her religious faith."[3]

The conceptualization of La Malinche as an Aztec Eve, a "traidora a la patria," a sullied whore who gave herself to the white conquistador, has been and still is reiterated by modern intellectuals. One only has to read the works of Octavio Paz and Carlos Fuentes focusing on La Malinche to realize the pervasive and corrosive nature of this stereotype.

The birth of the *mestiza* or Mexican woman began at the very inception of the conquest. Doña Marina's love for Cortés bore the children of the future — the mestizo race. Again, the role of the Mexicana has been stereotyped and presented as that of the submissive wife, the type of woman with absolutely no initiative to confront a swaggering and abusive *macho* husband; in fact, a woman with no educational or intellectual qualifications and whose only ability in life is to breed children. Thus, the stereotype of the "madre sufrida" emerges.

Needless to say, well-researched studies refute in no uncertain terms this characterization. Asunción Larvin's excellent collection of scholarly articles *Latin American Women: Historical Perspectives* (1978) indicates that woman's role was not that of mother and prostitute but extended to all facets of colonial society. To put matters in their proper perspective, everyone acknoweldges that the most outstanding figure in the colonial era was no other than a woman — Juana de Asbaje, most commonly known as Sor Juana Inés de la Cruz! Some thinkers and writers have tended to present Sor Juana as an aberration, even as a "monstruo de la naturaleza," but as more and more research comes to light we are getting a truer picture of women's activities during the sixteenth and seventeenth centuries. An increasing number of scholars are admitting that women were not cowering behind their husbands or cloistered in their homes but were instead an integral part of colonial society, participating in the marketplace as merchants and businesswomen, as "bankers" and property owners, and actively fomenting literary soirées.

It is indeed at a literary soirée that we encounter our next heroine, Doña Josefa Ortiz de Domínguez, whose involvement in the Wars of Independence (1810-1821) is now legendary. Dona Josefa's efforts in helping the revolutionary forces that were trying to throw off the yoke of Spain are well documented. It was her home that served as a meeting place for the insurgents to plot and execute their plans for an independent Mexico. The nation honors the memory of Doña Josefa by having her image imprinted on Mexican currency.

There is indeed a solid tradition of women's involvement in revolutionary movements. Yet the stereotype persists of the submissive, helpless female who does not know how to hold a pencil, let alone a gun. Historical facts again refute the stereotype. During the Mexican Revolution (1910-1917), Mexican women actively participated in the demolition of the old order and the formation of a new society. The "Adelitas" or "Juanas," as they are variously known, formed part of every revolutionary force. They were an integral part of the forces of Pancho Villa in the north of Mexico, of Emiliano Zapata in the south, and of Venustiano Carranza and Francisco I. Madero, to name a few. They marched with gun or rifle in hand or slung across their shoulders through the plains, deserts, and mountains of Mexico. Yet when the Revolution was over these valiant women were denied the vote on the grounds that ladies were not—or should not be—politically inclined! It was not until 1952 that Mexico saw fit to grant voting rights to women.

Marching throughout the pages of history we find women who refute time and again the worn-out stereotypes visited upon Chicanas and Mexicanas. Because of these conflicting sets of historical legacies—the stereotypical portrayal of the Chicana/Mexicana as whore-virgin-mother, contrasting with real-life experiences and historical personages that disprove the whore-virgin-mother triad—it is small wonder that many Chicana literary creations are concerned with a search for a "true" identity. The existential and philosophical questions of "Who am I?" and "What am I?" permeate the writings of Chicana autors; there is a quest that seeks to break out of the prison-like mold imposed from without which has sought to deny the Chicana's right to develop to her full potential.

There is, therefore, concern in the Chicana's poetic discourse to formulate, to conceptualize, to freeze in a moment of poetic intensity a new vision, a new perspective, a new definition of what the Chicana perceives herself to be. The cultural patterns imposed upon her will just not do for the present generation of women searching to redefine the cultural boundaries that have for centuries constrained them. Marcela Christine Lucero-Trujillo, for example, taunts her Chicano contemporaries in "Machismo is Part of Our Culture":

> Hey Chicano bossman
> don't tell me that
> machismo is part of our culture
> if you sleep
> and marry W.A.S.P.
> > You constantly remind me,
> > me, your Chicana employee
> > that machi-machi-machismo
> > is part of our culture.[4]

Silvia Alicia Gonzales, on the other hand, gags on the trivialization and stereotypes surrounding the word "Chicana":

> I am Chicana
> Something inside revolts
> The words surface with difficulty.
> I am Chicana
> By pronouncing this statement,
> do I give authenticity to the trivia
> which makes this statement me?[5]

Gonzales proceeds to explore the multifaceted meanings encompassed in the one word:

> I am Chicana
> Who dares to write letters
> given to me by a generous nun
> > . . .
> I am Chicana
> I am oblivion
> an appendage to the universe,
> a poverty statistic in life's data bank.
> > . . .
> I am Chicana
> Bastard child of the universe
> because you make me so.[6]

Sylvia's anguished poetic discourse explores the connections and interconnections between Latinas and other women and discovers that women in general are all Chicanas—i.e., second-class citizens.

> I am Chicana
> Latina, hispana americana
> does not your blood
> flow with the original sin
> of Montezuma's shame
>
>   . . .
>
> I am Chicana
> And I know my sisters
> I see you in Catholic confessionals
> reciting the same
> mia culpa, mia culpa, mia culpa.[7]

The historical relationship between the Chicana and La Malinche is reiterated throughout the poem and serves as a leitmotif to underscore the burden that modern day Chicanas/Mexicanas, the daughters of La Malinche, must bear because of this historical accident.

Gonzales closes her poem by asserting that whatever definitions and "misdefinitions" have been hurled upon Chicanas, her primary identity, the identity she chooses to embrace, is that of being a woman.

Likewise, Alma Villanueva, another outstanding Chicana poet, utters her poetic incantations in reference to her feminine identity:

> call me witch
> call me hag
> call me sorceress
> call me mad
> call me woman
>   do not call me goddess.[8]

The Chicana's search in literature for a cultural identity does not limit itself to the historical constructs emanating from a Hispanic/Latin American/Mexican experience but is also rooted in the conflictual situation in which she finds herself in United States society. The Chicana, a member of a "colored" race because of her mixed Indian and white ancestry, finds herself pitted against a racist society that refuses to recognize anybody as an "authentic," 100 percent American if she/he is not of "pure" Caucasian extraction — preferably Anglo-Saxon. Just as Chicanos have been burdened with a series of labels — Hispanic, Latin American, Spanish-American, Latino, Mexican-American, and other less palatable names — the Chicana has been labeled in a similar fashion. Rita Mendoza, first place winner of the Chicano Literary Contest (poetry section) at U.C. Irvine, 1974-75, comments on such an emotionally crippling pr in her poem "I'm a Chicana":

You could pass for an Anglo, they tell me if you tried
I said "I'm a Chicana," my head bent-down — I cried.
You could pass for a French girl, they tell me if you tried
I said "I'm a Chicana," eyes downcast — tried to hide.
You could pass for a Spanish, they tell me if you tried
I said "I'm a Chicana," eyes straight-ahead, sad, dried.
You could pass for a Chicana, no one has ever tried
I said "Thank you," my head held up with pride.[9]

The struggle to retain her Chicano identity is evidenced in the poetic enunciations of Marcela Christine Lucero-Trujillo:

Turn the corrido record down
    walk softly in ponchos
Speak Spanish in whispers
    or they'll approach you to say
    "I've been to Spain too, ¡Olé!"
    (even if you never have),
In Roseville, U.S.A.[10]

The fear of being culturally wiped out, of being assimilated, of her Chicana cultural specificity being denatured by the impinging vectors of prejudice and intolerance on the part of a conformist Anglo world, is interlocked in the lyrics of the above poem. The narrator perceives and feels the racist society surrounding her but does not surrender to the intimidating forces that seek to sterilize her, to straight-jacket her into white America's culture. The poetic persona of Lucero-Trujillo selfconsciously and dramatically asserts her right to be, to live in Roseville, U.S.A. — and to do it on her own terms. The scrutiny to which the narrator is subjected by the hostile eyes of a racist society only serves to concretize her Chicana identity and to awaken in her a political consciousness.

In this confrontational axis that pits the white race against the brown race there is no room for accommodation, and the dream of sisterhood shared by young white feminists is just that — a dream. Lucero-Trujillo perceives the gap between Chicanas and white women as being too wide to bridge, and the poet knowingly sputters in "No More Cookies Please":

WASP liberationist
you invited me
token minority
but your abortion ideology
failed to integrate me.
Over cookies and tea,
you sidled up to me
and said,
"Sisterhood is powerful"

> I said
> "Bullshit and allmotherfull"[11]

However, most Chicanas do share many of the concerns expressed by Anglo feminists. The early Chicano ideology of the 1960s condemned the Women's Liberation Movement as too divisive for Raza women to embrace; it saw the WLM as a threat to the integral cohesiveness of the group. Today, most contemporary Chicanos and Chicanas believe that women have to be liberated before complete equality is attained for both sexes. As María Inés Lagos-Pope points out in "A Space of Her Own: *The Second St. Poems* by Beverly Silva":

> In many ways, then, the Chicana is closer in her struggle for freedom and liberation to American women. . . . The Mexican or the Latin American woman has not attained the sexual freedom or the economic independence of her American counterpart, the Chicana in this case, nor does she enjoy the options available to the latter.[12]

Indeed, the liberated woman predominates in the thematic content of two contemporary poets: Beverly Silva, mentioned above, and Evangelina Vigil, author of *Thirty an' Seen a Lot* (1982). However, in both these authors the preoccupation with their Chicana identities, both vis-à-vis a racist society and as women in a sexist world, continues to lace their poetic discourse. Both Silva and Vigil seek to demolish in no uncertain terms the stereotypical images of Chicanas. Both poets employ a variety of strategies to convey their new awareness, their new status as liberated, educated, accomplished women. Vigil is the most forceful of the two with regard to language. By appropriating various traditionally male-reserved domains such as language and space (the barroom), Vigil generates a series of images that leave no doubt that the poetic persona enunciating the words in the poem has indeed "come a long way, baby." This is amply demonstrated in the poem "para los que piensan con la verga (with due apologies to those who do not":

> lost cause:
> ya no queda energía mental
> y ni siquiera señas
> del sincero deseo
> de tratar de aliveanarle la mente
> al hombre bien perdido
> en el mundo de nalgas y calzones
>
> se trata de viejos repulsivos
> de tapados con cobijas de asqueroso sexismo
> agarrándose los huevos

a las escondidas
with brain cells
displaced/replaced
by sperm cells
concentrating:
pumping away

ya no queda energía mental[13]

The traditional male linguistic preserves characterized by bawdy and "obscene" language, by the use of colloquialisms and street "jive," are no longer shunned by modern Chicana poets but figure prominently in their poetic discourse.

In spite of the stereotypes, there is a new voice seeking to assert itself in Chicano letters. Stereotypes need to be broken down. To this end the Chicana is taking the lead. Much, however, still needs to be done to improve the image of these women if we are to provide viable role models for future generations. In this respect, Chicana writers indeed can play a vital and pivotal role in extirpating the negative images they have been burdened with through the centuries. For it is the Chicana herself, above anyone else, who can explore the intricacies of her womanhood, her intimate self, and her soul and provide the world with a true image of who she is.

UNIVERSITY OF CALIFORNIA, IRVINE

Notes

[1] Alfredo Mirandé and Evangelina Enríquez, *La Chicana: The Mexican American Woman* (Chicago: University of Chicago Press, 1979), p. 59.

[2] Cited in Mirandé and Enríquez, *La Chicana,* p. 60.

[3] Adelaida R. Del Castillo, "Malintzín Tenépal: A Preliminary Look into a New Perspective," in *Essays on la mujer,* ed. Rosaura Sánchez (Los Angeles, Chicano Studies Center Publications, University of California, 1977), p. 142.

[4] Marcela Christine Lucero-Trujillo, "Machismo is Part of Our Culture," *The Third Woman: Minority Women Writers of the United States,* ed. Dexter Fisher (Boston: Houghton Mifflin, Co., 1980), p. 401.

[5] Sylvia Alicia Gonzales, "Chicano Evolution," *The Third Woman: Minority Women Writers of the United States,* p. 418.

[6] Ibid., p. 420.

[7] Ibid., p. 422.

[8] Alma Villanueva, *Bloodroot* (Austin: Place of Herons Press, 1982), p. 31.

[9]Rita Mendoza, "I'm a Chicana," *First Chicano Literary Prize Contest. Irvine 1974-1975* (Irvine, California: Department of Spanish and Portuguese, 1975), p. 81.

[10]Marcela Christine Lucero-Trujillo, "Roseville, Minn., U.S.A.," *The Third Woman: Minority Women Writers of the United States*, p. 404.

[11]Ibid., p. 402.

[12]María Inés Lagos-Pope, "A Space of Her Own: *The Second St. Poems* by Beverly Silva," introductory essay to Beverly Silva's *The Second St. Poems* (Ypsilanti, Michigan: Bilingual Press/Editorial Bilingüe, 1983), p. 18.

[13]Evangelina Vigil, *Thirty an' Seen a Lot* (Houston, Texas: Arte Público Press, 1982), p. 47.

References

Anton, Ferdinand. *La mujer en la América antigua*. México: Editorial Extemporáneos, 1975.

Barrera, Mario, Albert Camarillo, and Francisco Hernández, eds. *Work Family Sex Roles Language*. Berkeley: Tonatiuh-Quinto Sol International, 1980.

Barrett, Michèle. *Women's Oppression Today*. London: Verso Editions, 1980.

Beauvoir, Simone De. *The Second Sex*. New York: Random House, 1974.

Bornstein-Somoza, Miriam. *Bajo Cubierta*. Tucson: Scorpion Press, 1977.

Boxer, C. R. *Women in Iberian Expansion Overseas 1415-1815: Some Facts, Fancies and Personalities*. New York: Oxford University Press, 1975.

Bruce-Novoa, Juan. *Chicano Authors: Inquiry by Interview*. Austin: University of Texas Press, 1980.

Bullough, Vern L. *The Subordinate Sex: A History of Attitudes Toward Women*. New York: Penguin Books Inc., 1974.

Castillo, Ana. *The Invitation*. n.p.: 1979.

Cervantes, Lorna Dee. *Emplumada*. Pittsburgh: University of Pittsburgh Press, 1981.

Cisneros, Sandra. *Bad Boys*. San José, California: Mango Publications, 1980.

Cota-Cárdenas, Margarita. *Noches despertando inconsciencias*. Tucson: Scorpion Press, 1977.

Cotera, Martha. *Profile on the Mexican American Woman*. Austin: Information Systems Development, 1976.

————. *The Chicana Feminist*. Austin: Information Systems Development, 1977.

Del Castillo, Adelaida, and Magdalena Mora, eds. *Mexican Women in the United States: Struggles Past and Present*. Los Angeles: Chicano Studies Research Center Publications, 1980.

Díaz-Guerrero, Rogelio. *Psychology of the Mexican: Culture and Personality*. Austin: University of Texas Press, 1975.

El Grito: A Journal of Contemporary Mexican-American Thought. Vol. IV, No. 3, (Spring 1971).

Falcón, Lidia. *Mujer y sociedad: Análisis de un fenómeno reaccionario*. Barcelona: Editorial Fontanella, 1973.

Fisher, Dexter. *The Third Woman: Minority Women Writers of the United States*. Boston: Houghton Mifflin Co., 1980.

Fourth Chicano Literary Prize (1977-1978). Irvine, California: Department of Spanish and Portuguese, 1978.

Fuentes, Carlos, *Tiempo mexicano.* Mexico: Joaquín Mortiz, 1980.

Gallop, Jane. *The Daughter's Seduction: Feminism and Psychoanalysis.* New York: Cornell University Press, 1982.

García, Genaro. *Leona Vicario. Heroina insurgente.* Mexico: Editorial Innovación, S.A., 1979.

Hahner, June. *Women in Latin American History: Their Lives and Views.* Los Angeles: UCLA Latin American Center Publications, University of California, 1976.

Hoberman, Louise S. "Hispanic American Women as Portrayed in the Historical Literature Types or Archtypes." *Revista/Review Interamericana,* 4 (Summer 1974), pp. 136-47.

Hoyos, Angela de. *Arise Chicano and Other Poems.* San Antonio: M & A Editions, 1975.

—————— . *Chicano Poems for the Barrio.* San Antonio: M & A Editions, 1977.

—————— . *Selected Poems/Selecciones.* San Antonio: Dezkalzo Press, 1979.

Jaquette, Jane S. "Women in Revolutionary Movements in Latin America." *Journal of Marriage and the Family,* Vol. 35 (May 1973), pp. 344-54.

Jiménez, Francisco, ed. *The Identification and Analysis of Chicano Literature.* New York: Bilingual Press/Editorial Bilingüe, 1979.

Kessler, Evelyn S. *Women: An Anthropological View.* New York: Holt, Rinehart, and Winston, 1976.

La Cosecha/The Harvest: The Chicana Experience. Special issue of *De Colores,* Vol. 4, No. 3. Alburquerque: Pajarito Publications, 1978.

Lafaye, Jacques. *Quetzalcóatl and Guadalupe: The Formation of Mexican National Consciousness 1531-1813.* Chicago: The University of Chicago Press, 1976.

Larvin, Asunción, ed. *Latin American Women: Historical Perspectives.* Westport, Connecticut: Greenwood Press, 1978.

Leacock, Eleanor Burke, ed. *Myths of Male Dominance.* New York: Monthly Review Press, 1981.

MacCormack, Carol and Marilyn Strathern. *Nature, Culture, and Gender.* Cambridge: Cambridge University Press, 1980.

MacLachlan, Colin. "Modernization of Female Status in Mexico: The Image of Women's Magazines." *Revista/Review Interamericana* 4 (Summer 1974), pp. 246-57.

Martínez, Joe L. *Chicano Psychology.* New York: Academic Press, 1977.

Mestizo: Anthology of Chicano Literature. Special issue of *De Colores,* Vol. 4, Nos. 1 & 2. Albuquerque: Pajarito Publications, 1978.

Mirandé, Alfredo, and Evangelina Enríquez. *La Chicana: The Mexican American Woman.* Chicago: University of Chicago Press, 1979.

Mitchell, Juliet. *Woman's Estate.* New York: Random House, 1973.

Mujeres en revolución. La Habana: Editorial de Ciencias Sociales, 1978.

Okin, Suan Moller. *Women in Western Political Thought.* Princeton: Princeton University Press, 1979.

Oñate, María del Pilar. *El feminismo en la literatura española.* Madrid: Espasa-Calpe, 1938.

O'Sullivan-Beare, Nancy. *Las mujeres de los conquistadores. La mujer española en los comienzos de la colonización americana. Aportaciones para el estudio de la transculturación.* Madrid: Compañía Bibliográfica Española, 1956.

Paz, Octavio. *Sor Juana Inés de la Cruz o las trampas de la fe.* Madrid: Seix Barral Biblioteca Breve, 1982.

_____ . *The Labyrinth of Solitude: Life and Thought in Mexico.* New York: Grove Press, 1961.

Pescatello, Ann. *Female and Male in Latin America.* Pittsburgh: University of Pittsburgh Press, 1973.

_____ . *Power and Pawn: The Female in Iberian Families, Societies, and Cultures.* Newport, Connecticut: Greenwood Press, 1976.

Pettit, Arthur G. *Images of the Mexican American in Fiction and Film.* College Station: Texas A & M University Press, 1980.

Reiter, Rayna R. *Toward an Anthropology of Women,* New York: Monthly Review Press, 1975.

Reincourt, Amaury de. *Sex and Power in History.* New York: Dell Publishing, Co., 1974.

Rivera, Marina. *Sobra.* San Francisco: Casa Editorial, 1977.

Robinson, Cecil. *Mexico and the Hispanic Southwest in American Literature.* Tucson: The University of Arizona Press, 1977.

Robles, Mireya. *En esta aurora.* San Antonio: M & A Editions, 1978.

Rodríguez Baños, Roberto, Patricia Trejes de Zepeda, and Edilberto Soto Angli. *Virginidad y machismo en México.* México: Editorial Posada, 1973.

Rowbotham, Sheila. *Women, Resistance and Revolution: A History of Women and Revolution in the Modern World.* New York: Random House, 1974.

Sachs, Hannelore. *The Renaissance Woman.* New York: McGraw-Hill Book Company, 1971.

Sánchez, Rosaura. *Essays on la mujer.* Los Angeles: Chicano Studies Center Publications, University of California, 1977.

Sanday Reeves, Peggy. *Female Power and Male Dominance: On the Origins of Sexual Inequality.* Cambridge: Cambridge University Press, 1981.

Schneir, Miriam. *Feminism: The Essential Historical Writings.* New York: Random House, 1972.

Senour, María Nieto. "Psychology of the Chicana." *Chicano Psychology,* Joe Martínez, ed. New York: Academic Press, 1977, pp. 329-43.

Siete Poetas. Tucson: Scorpion Press, 1978.

Silva, Beverly. *The Second St. Poems.* Ypsilanti, Michigan: Bilingual Press/Editorial Bilingüe, 1983.

Soustelle, Jacques. *La vida cotidiana de los Aztecas.* México: Fondo de Cultura Económica, 1977.

Sponsler, Lucy A. *Women in the Medieval Spanish Epic and Lyric Traditions.* Lexington, Kentucky: University Press of Kentucky, 1975.

Stevens, Evelyn P. "Mexican Machismo: Policies and Value Orientation." *Western Political Quarterly,* Vol. 18, No. 4 (December, 1965), p. 848-57.

Third Chicano Literary Prize (1976-1977). Irvine, California: Department of Spanish and Portuguese, 1977.

Turner, Frederick. "Los efectos de la participación femenina en la revolución de 1910." *Historica mexicana,* Vol. 16, No. 4 (abril-junio 1967), pp. 601-20.

201: Homenaje a la ciudad de Los Angeles: Latino Experience in Literature and Art. Los Angeles: Los Angeles Latino Writers Association, 1982.

Van Hooft, Karen S. and Gabriela Mora, eds. *Theory and Practice of Feminist Literary Criticism.* Ypsilanti, Michigan: Bilingual Press/Editorial Bilingüe, 1982.

Vigil, Evangelina. *Nade y Nade. San Antonio: M & A Editions. 1978.*

_____ . *Thirty an' Seen a Lot.* Houston, Texas: Arte Público Press, 1982.

Villanueva, Alma. *Bloodroot.* Austin: Place of Herons Press, 1982.

Warner, Marina. *Alone of All Her Sex: The Myth and Cult of the Virgin Mary.* New York: Alfred A. Knopf, 1976.

Woll, Allen L. *The Latin Image in American Film.* Los Angeles: UCLA Latin American Center Publications, 1977.

Zamora, Bernice. *Restless Serpents.* Menlo Park, California: Diseños Literarios, 1976.

I. Prose

CHICANA NOVELISTS IN THE PROCESS OF CREATING FICTIVE VOICES

Francisco A. Lomelí

> "Your voice is lost to me, carnal."
> — Lorna Dee Cervantes

Chicano literature in the early 1980s finds itself at a precarious juncture, even in terms of the number of works being published. Some critics attest to a quantitative drop while others hint at a qualitative ascent. Within the body of Chicano literature, however, one fact remains constant: critical attention still lags far behind in proportion to the number of publications that have recently come to light. In fact, the modest boom of critical studies that proliferated during the 1970s has not made a significant impact on promoting new research to bring Chicano literature into some degree of world prominence or at least to the threshold of the American mainstream. Although remarkable gains have been made in this regard, Chicano literature seems to maintain some form of marginality among more traditional literary circles. If this assessment of its current status appears to be bleak, the picture becomes miserably amplified with respect to literature written by Chicanas, whose efforts have been generally ignored or misunderstood and stigmatized as being less rigorous in their approach to producing literature.

Chicana writers did not organize as an interest group until the special issue dedicated to "Chicanas en la Literatura y el Arte" in *El Grito* (1973).[1] This marked what Rita Sánchez later termed "breaking out of the silence"[2] and posited a critical stage of inner reflection in order to vindicate a historical gap that had endured and somehow gone undocumented for a long time. Chicana feminism had apparently gone unnoticed and the year 1973 can perhaps be regarded as the key point of departure for contemporary writings by Chicana authors whose inclinations were to accentuate an experiential perspective that focused on a woman's world view, her immediate sphere of social interactions, and concerns of a feminist nature. Thereafter emerged a series of special issues in journals addressing Chicana topics, and entire journals such as *Comadre* were created with the objective of providing a distinct forum to delve into issues earmarked by a particular interpretation and response that would differ considerably from both males and Anglo women. Literature written by Chicanas not only became a significant voice of the Chicano experience but also a mainstay in more contemporary trends with the purpose of breaking new ground and exploring further areas of human expression.

Thus far, Chicana poets have enjoyed some critical discussion, although they have not attained the same attention as their male counterparts. And, within this panorama of relative neglect toward Chicana creativity in general, the novelists have fared even worse as is evidenced by the alarmingly low number of critical studies devoted to novels written by Chicanas. True, this is partly attributable to the small number of female novelists, a total of four contemporary writers by the early 1980s: Berta Ornelas, *Come Down From the Mound* (1975); Isabella Ríos, *Victuum* (1976); Gina Valdés, *María Portillo* (1981); and Estela Portillo Trambley, *Trini* (forthcoming). With such a limited number of writers, it is no wonder that each writes strictly in her own individual style, thus avoiding any groupings or schools for followers. Their contribution as a whole has been to embark on portraying women as the central participants in a given situation as a natural outcome of their world view with respect to males.

The scarcity of Chicana fiction and its respective criticism seems to involve a variety of self-perpetuating factors. In terms of the actual numbers of works produced, there are those who point to the pressures of a society that essentially functions according to male interests in order to explain the inhibitors that discourage women, be it overtly or covertly. Some scholars, when pressed, allude to the limited availability of Chicana works by suggesting a lack of maturity in their ability to handle the craft of writing. As Evangelina Enríquez and Alfredo Mirandé state in *La Chicana: The Mexican-American Woman:* "Chicana literature . . . suffers from a lack of exposure in major publishing circles and is perhaps considered less than legitimate by some critics."[3] The writers themselves are aware, to varying degrees, of the psychological impact of writing in an unsupportive environment. If approached about why their novels receive minimal attention, the authors might answer confidentially that even Chicano publishing houses do not enthusiastically take the necessary risks with their works.

The psychological discouragement women writers are subjected to is carefully outlined by Eliana Rivero in a key article, "Escritura chicana: la mujer," where she posits a series of conditions particular to women as they are viewed as a socio-sexual class quite apart from and dominated by a male-oriented society:

> . . . la mujer *como grupo,* en paralelo a conjuntos raciales o sociales que históricamente no han estado asociados a la producción de 'Cultura', no ha tenido todavía la definición sociocultural requerida, la aprobación del código de costumbres y el tiempo de ocio necesario — con las sanciones y facilidades apropiadas — para una dedicación profesional a la escritura *de la misma forma en que la puede disfrutar el hombre.* El sistema aún no lo permite; sólo lo dificulta.[4]

The author proceeds to point out the sacrifices and commitment required by anyone involved in such intellectual endeavors; in addition, she also expounds on the additional demands placed on women labeled as "extrañamente agresivas" or accused of being of the inclinations "que no se avienen a su naturaleza femenina" when they achieve creative prowess. Here, the critic develops what Margarita B. Melville terms a situation defined as being "twice a minority";[5] Rivero believes that Chicano society restricts women's opportunity to fully exercise moral and mental independence by curtailing their "desenvolvimiento." She adds that if women manage to become intellectuals, "Son, en su mayoría, escritoras o creadoras o artistas o críticas que existen en el 'destierro espiritual' con respecto a sus compañeros de profesión . . ." (p. 5).

Social and historical factors, deeply rooted along sexual lines, have no doubt contributed to the view of woman's state as marginal in her milieu, thereby augmenting her relative exclusion from the main course of what male values deem significant. In literature, as in most activities, the effects on women tend to produce detrimental — although sometimes subtle — results, for example, in not being granted the same degree of legitimacy. In addition to this, the Chicana fiction writer is faced with another dilemma: the lack of a fundamental egalitarian relationship with male writers, forcing her to endure unfair and disparate comparisons with other authors. As Rivero explains:

> . . . hasta que estas variables no se controlen, hasta que la base material (y las actitudes culturales) sean iguales para escritores y

> para escritoras, resultará ilógico, 'antihistórico' (y ridículo) esperar
> el surgimiento de *una* Rolando Hinojosa, de *una* Tomás Rivera, de
> *una* Alurista, de *una* Rudolfo Anaya, de *una* Miguel Méndez. . . .
> Es un asunto de peras y de olmos. (pp. 7-8)

In short, literary criticism by Chicanos suffers from the same malady as its Anglo counterparts in not probing the creative production of women. And when Chicana works do appear they are rarely viewed critically to determine and decipher the author's intentions with respect to the literary standards they challenge. The underlying implication is that the issues women writers raise are not of great magnitude or importance. This conclusion can be easily verified by citing the astonishingly scarce bibliographical entries that deal directly with Chicana novelists.[6] The present study, then, attempts to remedy the obvious oversight on the part of Chicano criticism while focusing specifically on two novelists, Berta Ornelas and Isabella Ríos, who represent two distinct views on the art of narrating and whose works symbolize an attempt to create fictive voices.

Although our objective is not to resolve the differences between what critics consider male and female literature, a number of scholars have examined this controversial topic. For example, in *Sexual Politics* Kate Millett substantiates the claim that men and women do not represent separate species, but in many respects they represent separate cultures.[7] Research on the subject admits that works by women do not necessarily differ from those by men except in certain intangibles such as the role of feelings or patterns of self-perception or self-awareness — a variety of concerns of maximum interest to many Chicanas. Patricia Meyer Spacks, perhaps one of the more outstanding theoreticians on women writers, proposes conceptual delineations within what she terms "the female imagination,"[8] a provocative precept governed by a series of constants. She maintains that "Changing social conditions increase or diminish the opportunities for women's actions and expression, but a special female self-awareness emerges through literature in every period" (p. 3). To Meyer Spacks, the female novelist faces basically the same problems as any novelist, that is, she might be concerned with human relationships, personal identity, or the interchange between society and the individual. To this, she adds:

> Still, there appears to be something that we might call a woman's
> point of view — except that that sounds like a column in the *Ladies
> Home Journal* — a vague enough phenomenon, doubtless the result

mainly of social conditioning, but an outlook sufficiently distinct to be recognizable through the centuries. (pp. 4-5)

The author sees a pervasive socio-sexual class consciousness on the part of women writers in that likenesses among women are more fundamental than differences. This would have us believe that literature written by Chicanas qualifies more as female literature than as a cultural-historical component of Chicano literature. The implications are, of course, many and problematic in nature, thereby complicating the issue of what constitutes this body of literature. Within the same line of what Meyer Spacks puts forth, Simone de Beauvoir comments: "A man would never get the notion of writing a book on the peculiar situation of the human male. . . . A man never begins by presenting himself as an individual of a certain sex; it goes without saying that he is a man."[9] The general consensus would have us believe that the male view is the norm or standard by which to evaluate literature. If this is so, then literature becomes merely another medium through which to express — through symbolic means — power or politics by asserting one group over another.

Literature written by Chicanas is viewed from diverse perspectives: from those that stress its scant historical background to those that emphasize its recent composition as a variegated whole. Although new names are being discovered, only a few Hispanic women distinguished themselves in prose before the mid 1970s; among these are Nina Otero Warren and Jovita Gonzales, who concentrated on short stories and folktales. Meanwhile, poets were generally better known, mainly due to their sheer numbers, but most of them occupied only limited space in old newspapers and rarely achieved recognition. In the case of the long narrative, a New Mexican, Fabiola Cabeza de Vaca, was the first woman to receive some acclaim during her time for *We Fed Them Cactus,* published in 1954. A *sui generis* work which combines the chronicle and the novel, its focus is to recall *vaquero* days in New Mexico with a definite romantic tone of nostalgia; in it the author evokes the rough existence of ranch life and exalts the hard work of her people. Her literary acceptance, not by coincidence, is directly linked to her high economic stature among *hacendados* of her region, thus providing a retrospective view of *los de arriba.* Her orientation is not geared to exposing social conditions as they could have been, but rather she glosses over past history as if to justify and accept it. Despite her attitude of social acquiescence, some critics prefer to categorize her as an isolated case both as a woman writer and as an assimilationist. Her enigmatic persona becomes a moot point for she had no subsequent followers or emulators in her line of writing and left only a mild legacy by having intrigued readers with her work's title.

It is not until 1974 or 1975 — depending on whether we adhere to date of copyright or date of publication — that the first contemporary novel by a Chicana appears: Isabella Ríos copyrights her work *Victuum* in 1974 but publishes it in 1976, and Berta Ornelas makes her work *Come Down From the Mound* known in 1975. This sudden emergence of two novelists basically coincides with the International Women's Year of 1975, a key landmark when women around the world took significant steps to make their presence felt in all areas of social activity, literature being no exception. Ríos and Ornelas set out to break new ground by concentrating on the story rather than on style. Whereas 1975 serves as a focal point in time for Chicanas producing novelistic ventures, Marcela Trujillo argues in "The Dilemma of the Modern Chicana Artist and Critic" (1977) that the stage had already been set: "The impetus of the woman's movement together with the Chicano Movement contributed to the Chicana's latent potential and so she began to focus in on her particular feminist experience through the arts."[10]

Chicana contributions to novel writing aptly coincided with a key development in the Chicano novel in general that began in 1975, when an intense interest in experimentation effected new trends. Such novels as Ron Arias' *The Road to Tamazunchale* (1975) and *Caras viejas y vino nuevo* (1975) by Alejandro Morales revealed a new direction in narrative technique that corresponded more to what was in vogue in other world literatures. Through all of these efforts, the Chicano novel came of age; both subject matter and focus were structured to contort social reality with the objective of offering new images of the mental stage beyond the identity search that was previously evident in *Pocho* (1959) by José Antonio Villarreal and *The Autobiography of a Brown Buffalo* (1972) by Oscar Zeta Acosta. Among the dramatic changes that occurred, novelists examined a wide variety of social issues as they affect the individual, often relating situations to philosophical or ethical questions. The creation of community, as Tomás Rivera proposes, does not become a literary production in and of itself because the novelists after 1975, including Chicanas, sought to reshape archetypes of the sort that had been underrepresented in literature.[11] In this sense, cultural setting acquires less importance, for what matters above all is the dynamics of conflict between the individual and external forces. Ethnicity is no longer the ultimate aim but instead becomes a natural component of those who participate in the action. A conscious ideology of culture is now supplanted by the individual's circumstance as it becomes shaped and influenced by social agents. The result, then, is an internalized notion of self within a specific historical time in order to exhume a human drama of universal implications and regenerative possibilities.

Chicana novelists have made some significant strides in the aforementioned areas of experimentation in that they have expanded what Juan Bruce-Novoa terms the Chicano literary space.[12] They have, in fact, created women characters distinct from those of male authors by portraying females in ordinary and demythified roles. Their emphasis does not aim to idealize but rather to develop characters that offer some sense of verisimilitude as beings of flesh and blood. Even if their attempts have not been totally successful or convincing, it is difficult to deny that most protagonists in works written by Chicanas emanate a feeling of breathing a woman's "her-story" or situation.

Evangelina Enríquez and Alfredo Mirandé in *La Chicana: The Mexican-American Woman* make some worthy observations about literary expression by Chicanas in general that are also applicable to novelists. For example, they state: ". . . Chicana literature has probed deeper and more perceptively into the female situation and psyche than its American and Chicano predecessors" (p. 178). To this they add a comment on the achievements by Chicanas, although they do not specify the novel:

> Chicana writers address themselves to dilemmas of Chicano/American identity, male-female relationships, female roles within the family, and even female-female relationships. These subjects are marked by the intimate urgency of the first-person narrator in many cases; they refute prevalent stereotypes of women; and they allow for surprisingly lifelike characters in real-life situations. Interestingly, specific points in time and space — that is, either a historical backdrop or real locations — are not infrequently missing in Chicana writing. Landscapes or settings can be a more symbolic fabric against which characters and situations are played rather than real geographic entities. At the same time, personal experience and an autobiographical tendency in this fiction does away with detached accounts. Thematically, interfamilial relationships assume rich new dimensions; male-female relationships are conveyed via abstract expression and images; and the new frontier of female relationships is treated with astounding force that pushes back the literary perimeters American and Chicano authors have only begun to define. (pp. 178-79)

In effect, many of the aforementioned points make themselves manifest in the two novelists that are about to be analyzed.

Come Down From the Mound: Love and Politics

Aside from standing out as the first contemporary Chicana novelist, Berta Ornelas accomplishes another feat: her work, essentially political in nature, focuses on a present situation instead of dwelling romantically on the past, as was customary in previous writers. *Come Down From the Mound* (1975) unfolds the conflict between love and politics and shows how the protagonist seeks to reconcile the two. Aurora Alba, a young idealist and political activist, finds herself in the process of deciding whether to join the traditional political system or abandon it. Some background information is provided by an omniscient narrator who alludes to her previous militant tendencies when she was a student, showing her to be a reliable person to further a cause for social change.

When the novel opens, Aurora appears as a student-teacher in the position of making concessions to her beliefs in order to promote change from within the system. This represents the ideological backdrop of the novel as well as the personal crossroads for the protagonist. Her apparently virtuous principles, however, become muddled by ulterior motives relating to her romance with her adolescent idol, Jesús (Chuy) Santana, a twenty-six-year-old City Commissioner. The double-edged challenge symbolizes the struggle between the two young characters: Chuy wants to conquer her physically to satisfy the Don Juan in him, and by the same token he wants to claim her politically to secure yet another faithful follower. Most of the action involves this interplay of two people who commingle and talk beyond each other, thus accentuating their distinct approaches to using the political system for their own ends.

Some critics might dismiss the work as fluff, but it does have redeeming qualities on a variety of levels. As a political novel, it attempts to demonstrate how a small but growing empire can be infiltrated to change its priorities and, consequently, reduce the negative influence of power. Also, the work can function as a simple love story that a young reader might enjoy. Given its lack of breadth and narrative complexity, the novel is nevertheless effective in telling a story that is both political and romantic and in which either aspect can be regarded as the foreground or background. The convergence of the two opposing storylines allows the theme to emerge: love's capacity to conquer the evils of power.

The protagonist Aurora Alba, whose name embodies double idealism by symbolically repeating the concept of "dawn," seeks a new beginning to better days — or ways — in both love and politics. In her first appearance, Aurora functions as an omen to Chuy when she accidentally interrupts him in the act of massaging a pant-suited, buxom blonde in his office. The interruption marks the point when his licentiousness comes into question. Aurora, then, serves as the catalyst for his acquisition of a limited awareness of the boundless manipulations he enjoyed at the expense of women. While total reform might not be in sight for Chuy, the mere presence of Aurora Alba no doubt disturbs and curtails his free movement. She not only contributes to the breaking of his exploitation of women but becomes instrumental in weakening his position as a corrupt political figure. From the outset, the protagonist resembles in appearance a vestige of the militant 1960s, choosing faded blue jeans and a chambray shirt as an informal uniform so as to blend in with high school students. Aurora attends a campaign party for the young Chicano Commissioner, who soon becomes infatuated with her but then feels challenged by her indifference to his advances. Not accustomed to rejection, especially by women, he sets his sights on establishing a close relationship with her at all costs, as he says, "to find out what makes her tick."[13] What emerges is the characters' mental and attitudinal distance from life in general. Chuy feels mystified by her clouded nature, hidden impulses, calculating disposition, and feistiness; in other words, he views her as a true exception to the shallow simple-mindedness of the female lot he has known. She defies his mental construct and image of women while provoking his urge to re-evaluate and reach a new synthesis.

Chuy Santana, obsessed with acquiring political power, is a charismatic paladin whose influence extends to both sides of the border in a southwestern town, presumably in Arizona. His sphere of influence is such that he creates a small empire through astute and sometimes unscrupulous dealings with others from the dominant political structure. This idea is emphasized metaphorically in the novel in at least two ways: a drawing of the Pyramid of the Sun visually introduces each of the thirty-seven chapters, and numerous allusions are made to Santana's *cacique* qualities. On one occasion, Aurora remarks sarcastically:

> 'you must be one of those incarnate *dioses Aztecas*. Their *caciques* used to be considered incarnate gods. . . . The only thing that confuses me, though, is that the *conquistadores* were supposed to have decimated them all. But undoubtedly one of them got away. Tell me, how did you manage to give them the slip?' (p. 36, emphasis in the original)

Aurora, herself challenged, becomes determined to topple this self-made, political god, which clearly helps to explain the thrust of the novel's title. By contrast, Chuy Santana feels driven to accumulate wealth and property through any opportunistic means, justified by his desire to solidify his position in the community. With his self-serving goals, he seeks office for the lucrative gains of local politics. He admits openly that money figures as his ultimate hero and only guiding light, secondary to nothing. Santana comes to symbolize the political system and its resulting corruption, which breeds more of the same and relies on creating a network of loyal followers from whom to collect future favors, thus perpetuating a vicious circle. As Aurora points out, this form of politics distorts the virtue of loyalty: "that loyalty blinds a man. And that's the kind of loyalty you Chuy command. You thrive on it, you wallow in it. . ." (p. 163).

Aurora, having become an active member of the Cratican Party, learns the inner workings by which a political system coopts, corrupts, and diverts itself from those it aims to serve. Her idealism quickly comes in conflict with political reality, as her righteousness, civic pride, and concern for the poor are not enough to overcome the entrenched institutions that contain built-in mechanisms for self-preservation. She comes face to face with a fortified machinery of an almost invincible nature. Disillusioned as a consequence, yet uncompromising in attitude and deeds, the protagonist manages to win over Chuy Santana but not the system she sought to change. Her final victory entails lowering him from his pedestal, allowing him to succumb to love by renouncing his political career and his crooked ventures. While not prostituting her principles, she convinces Chuy not to prostitute his.

Although the storyline is usually developed in a shallow fashion, often containing more dialogue than action, the novel does include a definite female perspective on events. The perspective that dominates involves self-awareness through the undetached accounts of various women, some of whom still appear as stereotypes. Essentially, the novel focuses on Aurora, whose story reveals a multidimensional person involved in a series of conflicts and showing an assortment of psychological traits. Through her influence, she indirectly leads a group of female friends into a new consciousness that recognizes women's lot in society. Aspiring to become a writer—an almost gratuitous aspect of the work which is left hanging—she experiences a sense of liberation in planning to produce a book about sex, a subject she considers crucial to establishing egalitarianism between men and women. Her ideas never crystallize and remain undeveloped, perhaps due to the distractions she submits to. However, she verbalizes strong sentiments against marriage because she believes it to be an institution in which women are compelled to give more of themselves than men, and she views children as encumbrances to a possible career. The result clearly demonstrates that the protagonist equates male/female inequalities with the unfair and corrupt political system established by tradition. As the novel dramatizes women in diverse activities, it posits the notion that one needs to search for something other than what is considered the norm. Near the end, Aurora reaffirms an ideological position based on seeking new values when she says: "There are too many myths that have to be broken. It takes time to do that" (p. 244). In addition, she sees history as nothing more than a version of events by those who write it, implying that "herstory" has been relegated to a marginal status.

The novel suffers in other ways, especially in its confusion of identity labels; at times it opposes "Mexican" and "Chicano," denigrating the latter. At other times there is an attempt to gloss over ideological concerns so as not to appear dogmatic in the narrative. Also disturbing is the protagonist's idealization of her father while barely mentioning her mother, a point which becomes belabored and moot. Despite giving her mother little importance as a central figure, Aurora does mythify some popular women figures who have achieved a legendary status such as Adelita, Valentina, and María Josefa Ortiz de Domínguez. Some might argue that this view of women does not carry over into her daily interactions with other women and thus she falls victim to creating unnecessary hierarchies. Another debatable issue in the work is language: Spanish is dealt with as an oddity, almost excusing the Spanish-speakers for their speech by providing translations and at times mocking a nonfluent speaker who tries to communicate in English.

Despite some glaring weaknesses in handling the narrative, the novel contains a reservoir of valuable material for consideration with respect to women's treatment of love versus power. The narrator aims to discredit political structures and their cohorts as well as introduce revised concepts of femininity in relation to changing social roles. For once, some of the action and male characters are perceived through a woman's eyes and psyche, although this perspective is not meant to be understood as fixed but rather evolving in its own right. In the novel Aurora serves as the motor for potential change once she finds herself in a position to exercise her convictions and beliefs. In this way she represents those who assertively seek to institute fundamental changes on various levels: male-female relationships as well as political structures. But, above all, her greatest weapon is love, which she uses to instill in a man a voluntary recognition of fault, thus helping him acquire a new level of understanding toward women as well as a new sensitivity toward basic concepts of justice. The final question remains: who conquered whom? One thing is certain, the protagonist does not lose anything and Chuy substitutes his ambition with affection for Aurora.

Victuum: A Female Trajectory Toward Knowledge

In the second work, *Victuum* (1976) by Isabella Ríos, we have the first novel about psychic phenomena in Chicano literature, and it seems significant that a woman wrote it. The first *Bildungsroman* about a Chicana, the novel defies any single classification by expanding the scope of Chicano fiction in general. Its science-fiction quality somewhat resembles Arthur Tenorio's *Blessing From Above* (1973), whose thematic thrust deals with the intervention by an outer space being. Here, however, the main emphasis is on tracing a woman's "herstory" via the theme of traveling through life, an abstraction which becomes particularized by Valentina Ballesternos' own life story. Above all, there emerges a complete representation of a woman's psyche in its various stages of development within the metaphysical context of the universe. The storyline exemplifies a search for a cosmic self that goes beyond the cultural context of works such as ". . . *y no se lo tragó la tierra.*" Additionally, it can be regarded as a biographical novel about a woman who comes into contact with inexplicable phenomena. The work also demonstrates a close link with folkloric beliefs that border on magical realism through its acceptance of supernatural events and objects as ordinary happenings. The protagonist's physical and mental processes guide her trajectory of acquiring knowledge through external means at the same time that she becomes cognizant of certain powers of insight she possesses inherently through no volition of her own. If the narrative structure deals with her life story from the fetal stage to approximately fifty-five years old, its ultimate aim is to depict her mental prowess to the point where she experiences actual contact with beings from other worlds or other historic periods. This novel, *sui generis* in its composition, depicts a woman who transcends the physical world in terms of an outreach to other dimensions of knowledge, as if that realm were timeless and spaceless, that is, a dematerialized deposit or reservoir filled with ideas that exist in a type of fourth dimension. Women, or for that matter men, are not bound by physical demarcations, especially when these are viewed as merely temporary barriers to a person's potential for learning.

Victuum stands out as a unique work in light of the women's experience it reveals. For one, there is a definite intra-women social structure among the characters, most of which are females. There is a clear distinction made between the types of traditions women and men pass on to their children. Men, for example, involve themselves in relating familial stories, whereas some of the women express interest in matters dealing with unexplained phenomena. The other contrast can be seen in Valentina's father, who takes charge of household affairs while providing for the family; the mother, a housewife, does the household chores but also appears to function within her own realm. The mother concerns herself with issues she considers strictly feminine and passes them on to Valentina, who soon realizes that she has come to form part of a hushed network. The onion skin-like membrane she is born with, which resembles a thin veil, becomes the clue to this network. As Valentina matures, she discovers that she possesses innate powers of intuition and foresight, plus she can communicate or make contact with the dead and foretell future events. Her mother has similar abilities, thus creating a bond between the two as psychics, a fact the father is apparently ignorant about. These channels of communication rely on mental wave lengths and appear to exist only in women, although not all of them. The narrative emphasis is found in this mother-daughter relationship, due in great part to their abilities of insight. The novel does not aim to demonstrate that all women fit into this category, but it does imply that it is mainly women who do.

The female network in the novel exists as a means of exchanging information, impressions, and sometimes warnings. Its function is like an avenue through which events are dealt with almost in a clandestine manner, symbolically implying that society in general— perhaps male dominated—does not permit total development. Therefore, Valentina and her mother resort to separate means by which to express themselves about matters that are otherwise scorned by society. The novel, then, becomes a response to the urge to operate in this fashion, even if doing so is deviating from the norm. Valentina's world involves a clear separation between the physical and the mental, illustrative of a basic conflict she experiences. Reaffirmed by the novel's structure, also divided into two parts, Valentina's life is characterized by these pulls. The first part of the novel is an extensive account of her personal development from birth to young adulthood, occupying almost three-fourths of the entire book. The second part provides a quick overview of her adult years, approximately thirty years packed into one-fourth of the book. The first part presents her physical maturation process and the second her mental capabilities; the latter stage involves a search to become a whole person and somehow rid herself of the schizophrenic divisions.

Although the action in the novel bogs down in superfluous descriptions and innumerable humdrum occurrences, what emerges is the figure of a woman in the process of experiencing her surroundings. The narrative stresses the telling of a life story as it develops instead of presenting it from an omniscient point of view. The first-person narrator, Valentina, reproduces the action as she lives it, much like a camera would. This technique offers the possibility for the female narrator to divulge all that is seen and felt through her senses as she unravels events. The literary technique is designated by the use of quotation marks throughout the entire narration, that is, the action is completely dependent on Valentina as she perceives, thinks, or feels it. In this way, the narration becomes the protagonist herself as she relates her own story.

The issue of the fictive voice becomes even more complex when we attempt to reconcile the story of a psychic woman with that of the psyche of a woman. Here, various levels converge into what the author terms a "classical biographical novel," certainly a *sui generis* narrative that attempts to accomplish a number of objectives. For one, it aims to recount a real woman's life story after having conducted a series of interviews à la Carlos Castañeda. Then it tries to take the shape of a novel through the intercourse of fiction and fact, which is somewhat confusing because the empirical author (Diana López) assumes a semi-fictitious name (Isabella Ríos) at the same time that the main character (Valentina Ballesternos) supposedly represents a real person through another name. Cervantes would clearly have enjoyed these narrative disguises that obscure the real source of the story. Then again, we should perhaps ask if all of this is necessary. The complex makeup of the work reveals more about what it took to write it than it does about the nature of the story itself, except for the fact that the writer went to many painstaking efforts to juggle her various activities as compiler, transcriber, witness, actress, and, of course, novelist. Fortunately, the final outcome helps to situate the reader within the action and imagine it first-hand within Valentina's mind.

As strange as it might sound, the novel almost lacks a plot in the traditional sense because while it presents actions and events in a chronological order they seem to lead nowhere. The only thread is

Valentina herself, who in the end reaches a new height in psychic experience. The ultimate concern of the work revolves around Valentina's mental prowess; her physical development becomes secondary. For example, much of the first part deals with her coming to grips with her psychic insight by overcoming her fear of contact with another world. Of humble origins, she at first feels overwhelmed by her dreams and visions of people and things. She envisions family tragedies, specifically the deaths of relatives, and at no time does she seek to change the outcome. She passively permits the inevitable to occur in its proper time. Neither does she assume the role of informant because these experiences are nothing but indications of her future inclinations. Few events stand out in the first part of the novel, except when the fetus manifests itself as a conscience:

> My only regret is that I will begin life again. For as I sip nutrients from the soft warmth of my mother's breast, the knowledge I have gathered over centuries, epochs, will slip back into the sleeping silence of my conscience, and as my tiresome, limp fingers fondle the outer sustenance, it will be decades before they'll possess the strength to pull from the depths of my brain the knowledge of yesteryears.[14]

The significance of the excerpt lies in its suggestion of reincarnation, which implies that women perhaps represent the links in the cycle of life. In the novel, Valentina embodies a link of knowledge, for she speaks with people others have known only through books. From this point, especially in the second part of the novel, her mental trips become more frequent and, in fact, uncontainable. Because of the novel's ambiguity, it is not completely clear whether her visions are dreams or actual phenomena she sees, which further baffles the reader who tries to distinguish between the strata of reality. One of her first key contacts with a being from outside her immediate realm is with a warrior of God named Ulysseus (bringing to mind Ulysses), who expounds on the unbounded limits of the brain and guides her in a journey into the past. This could mean that the present and future can only be known by ascertaining the past. Her first encounter becomes an affirmation of life's cyclical nature in that a person's history marks a trajectory in the form of both physical and mental travels. As the cited quotation indicates, the person reaches mental maturity and, in a sense, returns to a permanent deposit of knowledge which is only mental. By this, the narrator Valentina implies that there exists a permanent present in the form of an eternal wealth of knowledge. To judge from the veil she was born with, she feels she has been chosen for the sake of knowledge.

Within a short span of time, Valentina's encounters increase, ranging from Medusa (who tries to vindicate herself for her evil reputation) to Aedauis (concerned with the total man and the fountain of youth) and from Pope Eusebius (who prefers a return to orthodox teachings in order to negate favoritism) to William Wordsworth (whose concept of style in concentrating on an eternal present reflects how *Victuum* is composed). The effect on the protagonist is that all of these encounters expand her concept of self; she now views herself as part of a long established continuum, which becomes a metaphor for history. Explained in abstract terms, she realizes that she forms an integral part of sound, the essential element that both announces and defines life. Her points of reference cease to be men or women but instead become the universe or human experience.

Whereas the historical and mythological figures she comes in contact with allow her to expand her horizons about knowledge as a permanent source, her final encounter with a planetary prince of knowledge named Victuum is the climax of the novel. This seems almost ironic, but most of all it marks the incessant search to surpass what people can offer the individual. As was stated in the early birth scene that "sound am I," the Mongoloid figure for whom the work is named now adds, "A child is not born of the child; a child is born of infinity" (p. 339). Her revelation is crucial for she realizes that she forms part of a cosmic framework instead of having to abide by dependent relationships with her fellow humans. Victuum's influence proceeds to open up her mental construct of the world even more, as he altruistically shares information and theories about abstract subjects such as sound, evolution, reincarnation, and time. A quasi philosopher, he assumes the role of mentor—much like Yoda did for Luke in *The Empire Strikes Back*—except that his *Deux ex machina* appearance lacks narrative substance. Victuum proposes concepts and theories, but he lacks any concrete knowledge about a system of values or guidelines to live by. His theoretical coldness more closely resembles computerized behavior, and he emphasizes the limitless potential of the brain, which again reaffirms Valentina's quest for knowledge.

The novel ends with virtually no action aside from the encounter with Victuum, giving the impression of an unfinished biography or a story uncertain of which way to turn. The protagonist remains filled with ideas and new notions about the universe but at the same time becomes confused about social issues, particularly miscegenation. Valentina achieves knowledge about abstractions while she loses sight of what this all means to her in concrete terms for her life. Finally, the novel functions on a variety of levels, a characteristic quite common in works written by Chicanas, allowing for various interpretations and a connotative purpose. *Victuum* aptly fits this trend, as if to imply that a woman's world consists of multiple roles and dimensions, or social obligations, quite apart from man's more unitary orientation. This in part explains the uncertainty evidenced in the fictive voice, who becomes exposed to new realms of knowledge yet does not know what to do with them. What clearly emerges is a different sense of history, or "herstory," as a composite picture of past and present. Besides, the protagonist does not only pay heed to physical things, for she gives credence to the metaphysical and the unexplained. Her notion of reality and existence is, in effect, more multifold.

Although our intention here has not been to establish canon on writings by Chicanas, there is no question that they offer new perspectives and nuances to Chicano expression. In both *Come Down From the Mound* and *Victuum* we find innovative approaches to depicting aspects of women's concerns or life experience. By examining the works in terms of the visions they present and the emotions they articulate, we can achieve a more holistic view of social complexity, breaking the monopoly that has been claimed by one sex. In the two novels analyzed, the authors propose the breaking of barriers, in one case political — aside from undermining *machista* traits — and in the other mental. These two novelists share the objective of portraying women in action as well as scrutinizing certain institutions and traditions. Their contributions lie in the focus and point of view on which they ground their story and with which they examine subjects in order to seek another synthesis, for their sake, in society.

UNIVERSITY OF CALIFORNIA, SANTA BARBARA

Notes

[1] This special issue is Year 7, Book 1 (September 1973), with Estela Portillo Trambley as contributing editor; it helped establish a sort of norm for subsequent efforts on Chicanas.

[2] The phrase expresses the author's thesis in an article of the same title which appeared in a special issue on the Chicanas in *De Colores* entitled "La Cosecha," 3, No. 3 (1977), pp. 31-37.

[3]Alfredo Mirandé and Evangelina Enríquez, *La Chicana: The Mexican-American Woman* (Chicago: University of Chicago Press, 1979), p. 178.

[4]Eliana Rivero, "Escritura chicana: la mujer," *La Palabra*, 2, No. 2 (Fall 1980), pp. 2-9. Despite its brevity, this article represents a seminal study for its polemic and comprehensive nature. Page references will follow immediately after the quotes cited.

[5]See Margarita B. Melville, *Twice a Minority: Mexican American Women* (St. Louis: C. V. Mosby Co., 1980), which contains a series of studies on a diverse cross-section of topics on the Chicana.

[6]The list may be summarized as follows: one review on Berta Ornelas' novel, one review and one article on Isabella Ríos' work, one interview on Estela Portillo Trambley with no in-depth studies on her forthcoming novel (this does not include the various articles on her dramatic pieces), and one brief critical assessment of Gina Valdés' writing. Surprisingly, this scarcity has not become a real issue to resolve, even among Chicana critics.

[7]See Kate Millett, *Sexual Politics* (Garden City, N.Y.: Doubleday, 1970).

[8]Patricia Meyer Spacks makes many worthwhile observations on women's creativity in her book *The Female Imagination* (New York: Knopf, 1975).

[9]These comments appear in Patricia Meyer Spacks' book *The Female Imagination*, p. 5.

[10]Marcela Trujillo, "The Dilemma of the Modern Chicana Artist and Critic," *De Colores*, 3, No. 3 (1977), pp. 38-48.

[11]See Tomás Rivera's article "Chicano Literature: The Establishment of Community" in *A Decade of Chicano Literature (1970-1979)*, eds. Luis Leal, *et al.* (Santa Barbara, CA: La Causa Publications, 1982), pp. 9-17.

[12]See Juan Bruce-Novoa's article entitled "The Space of Chicano Literature" in *De Colores*, 1, No. 4 (1975), pp. 22-42.

[13]Berta Ornelas, *Come Down From the Mound* (Phoenix: Miter Publishing Company, 1975). Page references will be given immediately after the cited excerpts.

[14]Isabella Ríos, *Victuum* (Ventura, CA: Diana-Etna Inc., 1976), p. 2. Other quotations will be indicated by their respective page references immediately after the citation.

THE FEMALE HERO
IN CHICANO LITERATURE

Carmen Salazar Parr
Genevieve M. Ramírez

The growing body of Chicano literature has created a wide range of characters who reflect the diverse aspirations, fears, and experiences of contemporary Chicano society. The characters portrayed in this corpus of literature emerge principally from the lower classes in an environment that is alien and hostile. Given the magnitude of the obstacles to be overcome in their struggle against the environment, the characteristic fortitude and endurance of these personages make their actions heroic in stature.

This study proposes to examine a selection of works that illustrate the heroic tradition within Chicano prose fiction with a particular focus on the female hero, a character whom we think has been largely overlooked. We believe that this figure warrants presentation in a new light, one that is reflected in the deliberate use of the term *hero,* as contrasted with the female "heroine" in works that are developed around the actions of a primary male protagonist. Our female hero, then, will exemplify those traits generally associated with the male literary hero. Additionally, the treatment of the hero figure will necessarily examine the unique aspects associated with heroism that emerge from the social and cultural realities of Chicano literature and of the Chicano experience it reflects. As Carol Pearson and Katherine Pope have noted, "until the heroic experience of all people — racial minorities and the poor as well as women — has been thoroughly explored, the myth of the hero will always be incomplete and inaccurate."[1] This study is one of the many studies called for in that challenge.

Perhaps the best and most precise treatment of the hero figure is

Joseph Campbell's *The Hero with a Thousand Faces,* in which he describes the hero-myth and discusses the psychological implications of numerous variations of the heroic quest. As Campbell explains:

> The standard path of the mythological adventure of the hero is a magnification of the formula represented in the rites of passage: separation — initiation — return: which might be the nuclear unit of the monomyth. A hero ventures forth from the world of common day into a region of supernatural wonder: fabulous forces are there encountered and a decisive victory is won: the hero comes back from this mysterious adventure with the power to bestow boons on his fellow man.[2]

Of course, each of the three principal stages identified above is executed in various substages or steps that begin with a call to adventure and culminate in reconciliation; collectively, they constitute a mythical journey. The hero undertakes this archetypal journey involving the confrontation of a "dragon" or an oppressive force, and he emerges either conquered or the victor, entitled to permanent joy and fulfillment. In the traditional sense, male heroes dominate the world they conquer; they display such characteristics as self-assurance, courage, and adventurousness. Campbell also declares that the hero may be male or female, the latter identified as goddesses, temptresses, or earth mothers. An important distinction is added by Pearson and Pope, who note that "an exploration of the heroic journeys of women — and of men who are relatively powerless because of class or race — makes clear that the archetypal hero masters the world by understanding it, not by dominating, controlling, or owning the world or other people" (pp. 4-5).

In dealing with ethnic minority and women characters as heroes, we observe certain basic differences immediately. First, the traditional hero rises from the upper classes or nobility and sallies forth from a position of strength and privilege. Because of the environment in which our nontraditional heroes move, their very beginning is from a social, economic, and cultural disadvantage that has resulted in alienation and disillusionment with God and man, with institutions, and at times with themselves. A second significant difference is the fact that the hero figure does not manifest all of the features usually associated with the hero-myth.

In our examination of the Chicana as hero we find this last characteristic to be predominant. In the relatively early works of playwright and novelist Josefina Niggli we observe the portrait of women in struggle. Her one-act plays leave no room for the development of the three basic stages identified by Campbell.

Josefina Niggli uses the Mexican Revolution as the setting in which her heroes move. That in itself is an interesting digression from tradition because women writers have generally concentrated on women's problems and issues, and they have usually avoided topics thought to be the concern and purview of male authors.

Niggli's 1936 play *Soldadera* portrays a female war hero in a manner that departs measurably from the romanticized images of the brave women who fought alongside their men in the Mexican Revolution of 1910.[3] It recounts the mission of a band of women soldiers to protect the rebels' ammunition. When a spy infiltrates their camp, feigning admiration for the revolutionary cause, young Adelita is his chosen target because of her youth and presumed vulnerability. It becomes the task of Concha, the group's leader, to devise a scheme to uncover the means by which the spy is successfully transmitting messages back to the *federales*. The execution of the plan requires the sacrifice of one of the women, who will effectively commit suicide by throwing a landslide-producing bomb. Surprisingly for the women themselves, in the final outcome the intended hero (the Cricket) is stopped by a paralyzing fear of death and it is Adelita who assumes that role without any hesitation.

The general similarities between Niggli's portrait of the Mexican Revolution and that offered by Mariano Azuela in *Los de abajo*, though not the principal topic of this discussion, are too striking to overlook. Niggli dramatizes the same events as Azuela and does so utilizing some of the same stylistic devices in naming and characterizing fictional creations;[4] interestingly, however, she chooses to focus on the contributions of women to the revolutionary cause.

The play really depicts two female heroes. The more extensive portrait is that of Concha, the unquestionable leader of the band of women soldiers. She is admired by the women she leads and even by the enemy (the male federal spy) because she exhibits traits not generally associated with or expected of women. Her realism springs from the fact that she can be both a loving individual and a hardened woman, as circumstances demand. Niggli describes her thus:

> As dirty as the rest of them, there is strength that flowers in her body and sets her above and beyond them. Born of the earth, it is the earth's pulse that she has for her heart. She is the one who keeps those fighting, snarling women together . . . who can punish with a sure, cold hand, but at the same time can heal their wounds. As merciless as the wind and rain, she is as warm and healing as the sun. (p. 74)

One of the typical elements in Niggli's plays is a discussion of deeds appropriately executed by male and female characters. In *Soldadera* that exchange involves Concha, who is challenged by the captured spy when she contemplates torturing him because, he maintains, women should be incapable of such acts. Her reply eradicates any real distinction between the sexes when both are forced to confront the same dehumanizing realities: "Are we women? Sometimes I wonder. The Old One cooks our food . . . she saw her son crucified by men of your kind . . . another one saw her son hunted down by dogs for the sport of it. That doesn't make women, my friend. That makes something worse than the devils in hell" (p. 94).

The other female hero in the play is Adelita, who emerges as such only in the final scene. Niggli creates a striking contrast between Adelita and the Cricket, who speaks harshly and advocates a drastic course of action but cannot deliver the self-sacrifice when called upon to do so. Adelita, the uncorrupted one, becomes the hero in a spontaneous but deliberate response to circumstances. Her courageous confrontation of death makes her a hero because, as Campbell notes, "the last act in the biography of the hero is that of the death or departure. Here the whole sense of the life is epitomized. Needless to say, the hero would be no hero if death held for him any terror; the first condition is reconciliation with the grave."[5]

There exists a certain similarity between Adelita and the mythological Ifigenia; both are innocent and sweet, and willing sacrifices for a noble and necessary cause. However, it is important to note that Adelita is not the involuntary sacrifice whose fate is externally determined (Ifigenia was beheaded because of her father Agamemnon's decision) but rather the conscious determiner of her self-sacrifice for a freely embraced cause. Niggli's women are not the stoical *mujeres sufridas* (women who are submissive to a social station imposed by a male-dominated society and their maternal obligations); instead, their form of self-sacrifice is their deliberately assumed role as active agents for change.

In *The Ring of General Macías* (1943) Niggli touches again on the theme of the Revolution but makes the dramatic situation revolve around the conflict experienced by those who are torn between love for country and love for an individual.[6] This one-act play begins with a quote from Joaquín Peralta's *Essay on the Great Revolution:* "The Federal troops were fighting for a way of living; the Revolutionists were fighting for life itself. The outcome for such a struggle could never be in doubt" (p. 144). This point becomes the subject matter from which Niggli develops the plot for her play. The central figure is Raquel, wife of the Federalist General Macías; she ends up sympathizing with the revolutionary spirit once she recognizes that Andrés and Cleto, the two spies who force her to give them refuge, show more courage and love for country than her prisoner husband does. To save his own life "because of his love for Raquel," General Macías allows the spies to seek refuge in his own home.

The Ring of General Macías is a play about honor and love, but here it is the woman who sustains that honor, both for herself and for her husband, who is considered by others to be a coward. In the dialogue between Raquel and Cleto it becomes clear that honor is thought by men to have a different meaning when applied to themselves than it does when applied to women.

Raquel:	And so is my husband a great man. He is of the family Macías. All of that family have been great men. . . . They have always held their honor to be greater than their lives. That is a tradition of their family.
Cleto:	Perhaps none of them loved a woman like you, señora.
Raquel:	How strange you are. I saved you from the Federals because I want to save my husband's life. You call me brave and yet you call him a coward. There is no difference in what we have done.
Cleto:	But you are a woman, señora.
Raquel:	Has a woman less honor than a man, then?
Cleto:	No, señora. Please, I don't know how to say it. The general is a soldier. He has a duty to his own cause. You are a woman. You have a duty to your husband. It is right that you should try to save him. It is not right that he should try to save himself. (pp. 158-159)

In the final scene Raquel poisons the captain's wine, fully aware that his death will mean the death of her husband. She thus saves her husband's honor and, although recognizing that the Revolution will win in the end, she prevents the information about the battle from leaking out. She does not try to save her husband's life because it is a nobler and more honorable deed to uphold the cause (thwarting the Revolution, since she is an aristocrat) than to protect the husband she loves at the expense of the cause. Once again the roles have been inverted and the final outcome is left to the conscious choice of the woman.

In this case, what prompts the heroic act on Raquel's part is her encounter with an outside agent whose strong commitment to an alien political ideology takes her from passive acceptance into action or energy. In the quest, as discussed by Campbell, there is a passage from innocence into experience. That process is precipitated by a call to adventure, represented in the play by the intrusion of Cleto and Andrés into the Macías home. It is these characters who, having issued the call, guide Raquel through the process of reconciliation with truth. Raquel's blind allegiance to the Federalist cause and faith in her husband's courage and honor are challenged by Cleto's disdain for General Macías' cowardice; it is her realization of that truth that motivates her decisive defiance of her husband's presumed wishes and expectations. This is essentially the same process experienced by Adelita in her transition from innocence to mature action. Furthermore, Raquel's allegiance to the Federalist cause is shaken considerably in her admiration for and openness to Cleto's ideology. Ironically, even though she feels compelled to poison Cleto, she succeeds simultaneously both in upholding her husband's honor and in removing him as an oppressor of the insurgents.

It is clear that Josefina Niggli's ideological posture is support for the Revolutionary cause. In presenting the conflict, however, she creates heroic women figures who rally in both camps. What is important is that her female heroes take their stands not for personal self-aggrandizement but as actors in a collective effort for the common good.

Quite the opposite is true in Estela Portillo Trambley's works, written some forty years later, where the female hero often seeks personal gain. There remain, however, some important parallels between the creations of Niggli and Portillo Trambley. Both focus on woman's ability to defy the stereotypical restrictions on her role and freedom in society, stressing characteristics of women as women. Death usually remains an outcome for the hero and at times for others. Elements common to both writers become evident in an examination of Nina, the female hero of Portillo Trambley's short story "The Trees."

Married to the youngest son of the Ayala family, Nina undertakes a quest for justice by attempting to gain her husband's rightful share of the family apple orchards. In championing that cause she confronts and slays its particular "dragons," namely the older brothers who, in birth order, control the family orchards. She thus creates conflicts among the brothers so that they destroy one another. Having completed that objective, she ends her own life.

Nina's true rebellion is directed against the restrictive, carefully patterned lifetyle of that social order, reflected concretely in the patrimonial family structure and laws of inheritance, in lives that "were well patterned like the rows of apple trees and the trenches that fed them."[7] She refuses the voiceless, powerless insignificance bestowed on the women of Cetna.

Nina's heroism derives essentially from her daring defiance of tradition, but her characterization is more ambiguous than that of any of Niggli's figures. The narrator describes her as Eve and the serpent (tempting and entrapping her brothers-in-law), the apple, and an avenging angel. Her extreme solution of violence and destruction is presented as a necessary prelude to desirable change. Her final act of defiance, the fatal plunge from a hill which effectively ends the plot, is given two interpretations. On the one hand, it is described as an act of personal liberation, as the means of achieving freedom from male dominance in a still oppressive society. Nina looks forward to reaping "a good harvest in Paradise" (p. 21) solely for her personal benefit. Nevertheless, the narrator's interpretive comments make it very clear that Nina's chosen death is also, like Adelita's, a sacrifice that will be collectively beneficial. It is the final step in a destructive process without which the new order cannot come into being. The final image in the story is one of barren desolation that seems to await the creation of new life.[8]

Nina's heroism, not unlike Concha's in *Soldadera,* resides in her willingness to replace the expected feminine gentleness and tenderness with the stereotypically male harshness and violence demanded by the quest she undertakes. She, like the band led by Niggli's Concha, has known "inhumanities and cruelties" (p. 13) that cannot be erased from her consciousness. Both writers demonstrate that when women assume traditionally masculine traits, the invariable result is destruction.

A similarly cruel past is responsible for Beatriz' hardened character in Portillo Trambley's "If It Weren't for the Honeysuckle." Beatriz is depicted as a woman who has patiently endured a pattern of alternating abuse and abandonment by her husband Robles, deriving her pleasure of accomplishment from the construction and improvement of a house and the meticulous cultivation of an orderly, manicured garden. Her tolerance continues as she cares for a younger woman Robles leaves with her until he arrives with a very young, abused girl. At this juncture she determines that he cannot be permitted to continue in that pattern and plots to kill him by poisoning his soup. In his death and burial beneath the honeysuckle vines these women are freed from his tyranny as are the unknown prospective victims spared from his abuse.

Like Nina, then, Beatriz emerges as a rebel against an oppressive social order. Unlike Nina, however, she is a proponent of order and balance: "Beatriz knew it was up to her to find and keep an order as she had always done. She must add and subtract the reality of things" (p. 103). What emerges in this story is the clash between her sense of order as it should be and Robles' imposition of the established order reflecting the man's point of view. Heroism in Portillo Trambley's works, as in Niggli's, resides in the determination to respond to harshness and restrictiveness of circumstances in the only ways possible, by daring to resort to extreme measures. Clearly, these women are not the lovely heroines who serve to highlight the merit of a male protagonist; they are heroes who define and unrestrainedly pursue a mission that will ultimately have a significant impact on others. Submission to circumstances or escape would not be considered heroic responses. Their violent alternatives are not upheld as an ideal worthy of imitation but as the only viable means of effecting change. Nina's death is an act of transcendence and Beatriz' murder of Robles signifies liberation from oppression.

A contrast to the two preceding figures is represented in a very positive female hero figure, Clotilde Romero de Traske of Portillo Trambley's "The Paris Gown." Clotilde's "dragon" is also social convention, specifically her father's right to arrange a marriage for her. Since she perceives marriage as a kind of slavery that would stifle her creativity, she devises a scandalously daring plan (a naked appearance before the wedding guests) that allows her to go live in Europe, where she has the freedom to pursue her artistic interests.

Clotilde's recognition of a solution to her problem and her response to that inner voice are what make her a hero rather than a victim. As explained by Pearson and Pope, that voice of affirming worthiness, potential happiness, and capacity to acquire it are for the female hero the equivalent of the classical hero's call to adventure and departure.[9] Clotilde tells her granddaughter: "One morning I awoke knowing the answer to my problem . . . I simply had discovered a way out" (p. 7). Like Beatriz, then, she responds to a commanding impulse from within, and does so calmly and carefully. Where Clotilde differs markedly from her sisters in the world of Estela Portillo Trambley is in her tolerant and sympathetic attitude toward men. She sees them, too, as dominated by a more powerful social order: "Men have attempted fairness since the beginning of time; it's just that sometimes they are overwhelmed" (p. 3).

That understanding appears to be the result of a very different set of circumstances, especially her successful escape from a potential agent of the old order (her father) before he could become an active oppressor. She does not seek to change the dominant circumstances but only to find alternatives. Unlike the characters discussed previously, she escapes the drive for power that seeks to violently overthrow the existent authority. Her sole objective is to control her own life and she is able to do so without assuming male characteristics, retaining the essentially feminine intuition, sensitivity, and creativity. Her successful transition is symbolized by her departure from her father's very symmetrical garden to establish a new order and a new garden in Paris which are her own original creations.[10]

The desire to exercise control over one's own life is sometimes a deliberate choice; at other times it is the result of circumstances. But whether the actions represent a conscious choice or not, women do embrace the opportunity for self-determination wholeheartedly. What they aspire to is independence from men.

Gina Valdés' novel *There Are No Madmen Here* offers an example of the involuntary effort toward independence.[11] María Portillo's call to action occurs when her husband abandons her in Mexico with three high-school-aged daughters, living in a shack that only miraculously stands against the elements. Her struggle to overcome poverty is executed through a "journey" across the border to the United States, where she secures a meager living in a factory and eventually becomes involved in a family business smuggling tequila across the border. That illegal activity is hardly virtuous, but the author's portrayal of the situation is understanding. This account is not a fairy tale but the representation of a very real situation confronted by thousands of men and women struggling to secure life's basic necessities for themselves and their families.

The characters created by Valdés are the ordinary human beings we meet in everyday life, unlike Estela Portillo Trambley's essentially typecast, romanticized figures. Valdés' characters are truly multidimensional; they experience any number of setbacks and tragedies and suffer because of them, but they also manage to retain a sense of humor and to find opportunities to enjoy what they do have. Deserted by a husband who has literally gone mad, thinking himself the reincarnate poet-king Nezahualcóyotl, María is still able to joke about the advances of an old friend who is now courting her: "He's a good man, but he could change. . . . He might want to come and go like Efrén, and once again I'd be the one who's expected to wait. I can see it happening, Miguel deciding he was Moctezuma and going off to Yucatán to join Efrén. It could be worse. He could decide he was Moctezuma and not go away" (p. 108).

Lighter observations and a sprinkling of humor in the face of catastrophe maintain the predominant optimism and prevent the work from reaching tragic dimensions. In the final segment María's brother is persuaded to include six parrots in his camperload of smuggled tequila; he gives the birds liquor to put them to sleep while he crosses the border, but one of them doesn't succumb and his deception is discovered:

> "I thought I heard something."
>
> "I didn't hear anything."
>
> (Viejo cabrón)
>
> "It sounds like a woman's voice . . . it sounds like it's coming from the back of your camper . . ."

When María is called by her brother, she reacts as the reader does:

> "Ramón? where are you? Oh, no, how did it happen? What? Are you joking? You're not joking? You were turned in by a parrot? Oh Ramón, and by a parrot!" (p. 151)

Because this novel deals with contemporary socioeconomic realities, the quest represented is first for survival; secondly the struggle is for betterment of the basic life experience and opportunities. María's passage from innocence to knowledge is the realization of her permanent abandonment by her husband; i.e., she recognizes that the state she had embraced, seeking security, has failed to provide her with it. Her first response is a highly symbolic act, the burning of her wedding dress. From that impulse she derives a strong feeling of relief, energy, and the confidence that she can do whatever she chooses (p. 50). That immediate choice is announced suddenly to her daughters: "We're going to live in the United States" (p. 50).

María's departure requires that she give up the symbol of marriage, which is usually the most tenaciously retained. At the Tijuana border she sells her wedding ring to secure bus fares for her family to Los Angeles, where she plans to stay temporarily with two aunts. Arrival creates a new dependence on those very domineering individuals. Thus, her problems are not solved in the first step of transition, but her determination to provide a better life for her daughters remains a powerful motivation and she escapes that new-found tyranny as quickly as possible.

By the close of the novel, María has entered a different socioeconomic reality, which carries with it its own problems. One of her daughters aspires to attend law school in the East, but another marries an Anglo who disdains anything Mexican, and the third

follows her boyfriend to Japan. Regardless of whether their choices
are good or bad, it is obvious that the next generation faces changes
and opportunities that their mother lacked. There is a distinct possibility that they will follow their mother's example of departure in
pursuit of personal quests.

The ambiguity of that outcome is mirrored in the entire book: the
tequila is María's financial salvation and her brothers' instrument of
self-destruction (alcoholism); Los Angeles is the land of opportunity
and an opportunity for perdition, and so on. The modern hero is not
a superhuman being, and life is neither black nor white but shades of
gray. In Portillo Trambley's stories the characters struggle to escape
reality and secure the freedom of the creative world (Clotilde, Nina,
and many others). Gina Valdés has created the converse in this novel.
Women characters are usually portrayed as insane, but here it is the
husband who lives in the creative, intuitive world of books. The
woman is left to bear the burdens of the real world by a man who is
unable to reconcile his desires with reality. That real world is the
socioeconomic circumstance of the southwestern United States and
Mexico. As the reversed roles are a matter of fact, so too the changes
experienced in the transition from Mexico to the United States are
positively accepted; there is no nostalgia for the homeland or its
traditions. It is within this context that the female heroic qualities
must be defined and examined.

Poverty, or the need for survival, is also the driving factor in
Estela Portillo Trambley's (forthcoming) novel *Trini*.[12] This work
traces the life of its title character from early adolescence to stable
adulthood through a series of catastrophes that mold her into the
mature person she eventually becomes.

Trini's transition from her unconscious quest for the impossible to
reconciliation and self-realization takes her through a series of
negative experiences. What she seeks is the ideal circumstance in
which she had seen her mother: land, a home, and her family united
and supported by a hardworking, faithful, and loving husband. The
death of her mother and her father's transfer to a mining job elsewhere, followed shortly by his hospitalization for tuberculosis, plunge
Trini into a prolonged search to regain the stability of the past: "Yes,
yes, her heart said, run, find the days now gone, find the old, honey
golden expectations" (p. 268). She is driven by her love for Sabochi,
an idolized (and idealized) Indian who had helped to raise the
children after their mother's death. Although he marries a woman
from his tribe, his loving relationship with Trini is presented as a
pristine perfection to be sought despite its deviation from social
convention.

In day-to-day reality, however, Trini is raped, has a child who dies soon after birth, and is seduced by Tonio, the man who had accompanied her family in relocating to the mines. She is abandoned by him before their first child is born, but he will return and depart several more times. She leaves her daughter with friends to seek income for survival, finds Sabochi for a brief interlude from which her first son is born, loses Tonio's love to her best friend, who rejects him, and — many experiences later — acquires a plot of land on which she and her five children eventually settle and where her father joins them after his recovery. At the close of the novel she realizes that she can experience fulfillment and contentment through the land and her family but without the protection and provision of Tonio, and without Sabochi.

Trini's quest for fulfillment remains an unconscious one through most of the novel. In the last third of the work, as she awaits the encounter with Sabochi, she is questioning her own desires: " 'What do I want? What am I doing here? Why do I run and look and search and never find? . . . What forces drive me like the earth?' A fierceness seemed to rise in her, mute, indistinguishable. It was a folding inward, the mind grappling for answers, for reasons" (p. 269). Shortly afterwards, as Sabochi hands her a moonstone as a gift, she recognizes an important parallel: "It was her papa offering a silver happening to Matilda because he loved her. Sabochi loved her. It was in his face" (p. 273). His parting gift forces her to relinquish her dreams of a future with Sabochi, but she is still driven by the quest for her mother's life.

Trini's desire to purchase land leads her to the border to work in El Paso, an episode that most clearly resembles the socioeconomic realism of Gina Valdés' novel. Here, too, the view of the United States as the land of opportunity is reflected in Trini's determination to bear her second child in the United States so that he may use his rights as a citizen and so that she may use the circumstance of his birth to realize her own objectives: "All she wanted was a chance, a way to stay in the United States, the finding of a piece of land, the family together" (p. 352). Ultimately, she does acquire the land and does unite her family under her own strong leadership, finally planting the packet of her father's seeds which she had carried for years while awaiting a permanent place to reap their harvest.

Trini's quest closely parallels the heroic journey to self-fulfillment as summarized by Pearson and Pope (p. 68). The first stage, which they term "the exit from the garden," is an escape from initial dependence, but the hero moves from that stage into "the emperor's new clothes," where a seducer, another captor, introduces the dragon of romantic love. Trini's release of Sabochi to return to lead his tribe slays that dragon. In the final stage, "A woman is her mother," the hero achieves wholeness by recognizing that traditional male sexuality and independence are also hers; she is freed from the myth of female inferiority. "The child had been burned out of her . . . The journey was over, the land had been found, the family had been gathered" (p. 387).

The evolution represented in the journey is paralleled by her mythological identification as mother-earth figure; her own comments about Tonantzín imply that she sees herself closely associated with the goddess. She appears through most of the novel as an unreal figure, the caring mother, the forgiving victim of male-inflicted abuses. Nevertheless, at the close of the novel she finally rejects Tonio because of his betrayals of her; no longer the idealized symbol of selflessness, she is now a human being who will not tolerate what must rightfully be rejected or avenged.

We have sought to explore the hero myth as portrayed in Chicano literature, specifically within the context of works written by women about women. The myth, then, is situated in circumstances unique to the cultural bases of the minority group that produced it; it functions within that ambiance without extending to include rebellion against the dominant (Anglo) culture that oppresses or constrains the ethnic minority group as a whole.

We have found that in these female-authored works women exhibit the same heroic qualities as men, as described by Joseph Campbell. The "dragons" challenged by women are the conventions created in a male-dominated world. Perhaps the foremost heroic achievement resides in the assumption of those heroic qualities, possible only in the conscious deviation from the traditionally feminine characteristics imposed by men. Our women heroes do not, however, seek superiority and dominance but rather parity and equality of stature, respect, and opportunity. Clearly, they are neither the traditional heroes in positions of power nor the traditional heroines whose roles support the heroic achievements of men. Hence, our use of the term "female hero" in the examination of these characters.

LOS ANGELES VALLEY COLLEGE

CALIFORNIA STATE UNIVERSITY,
  LONG BEACH

Notes

[1]Carol Pearson and Katherine Pope, *The Female Hero in American and British Literature* (New York: R.R. Bowker Co., 1981), p. 5.

[2]Joseph Campbell, *The Hero with a Thousand Faces* (Princeton: Bollingen Press, 1949; rpt. 1973), p. 30.

[3]Josefina Niggli, *Mexican Folk Plays* (Chapel Hill: University of North Carolina Press, 1938). Citations from this play are taken from this edition.

[4]Such characters as the Blond One or the Cricket clearly recall Azuela's güero Margarito or la Pintada; similarly, both authors ascribe animal-like behaviors to their personages. The reader would also note a resemblance between Adelita's treatment of the Rich One and Camila's relationship to Luis Cervantes in Azuela's novel (note, for example, their conversation in Part I, Chapter 11 of *Los de abajo*).

[5]Campbell, p. 356.

[6]Josefina Niggli, *The Ring of General Macías,* in *20 Prize-Winning Non-Royalty One-Act Plays,* comp. Betty Smith (New York: Greenberg Publisher, 1943). Citations from the play are taken from this edition.

[7]Estela Portillo Trambley, *Rain of Scorpions* (Berkeley: Tonatiuh International, Inc., 1975), p. 13. Subsequent citations from Portillo's short stories are taken from this edition.

[8]For a discussion of Nina as tragic hero see Patricia and Vernon Lattin, "Power and Freedom in the Stories of Estela Portillo Trambley," *Critique,* 21, 1 (Fall 1979), pp. 93-101.

[9]Pearson and Pope, p. 83.

[10]We have not discussed the quest manifested in Portillo Trambley's "The Pilgrimage," which (of the stories in this collection) most completely embodies the hero myth, because of María Herrera-Sobek's detailed analysis of that story in "La unidad del hombre y del cosmos: reafirmación del proceso vital en Estela Portillo Trambley," concurrently in preparation for the forthcoming *Homenaje a Luis Leal* (ed. Francisco Lomelí).

[11]Gina Valdés, *There Are No Madmen Here* (San Diego: Maize Press, 1981). Textual citations are taken from this edition.

[12]*Trini* will be published in 1985 by Bilingual Review/Press. The citations in this study are from an early draft of the novel, which had the working title *Woman of the Earth.*

CHICANA PROSE WRITERS:
THE CASE OF GINA VALDÉS
AND SYLVIA LIZÁRRAGA

Rosaura Sánchez

The literature of Chicana female writers can only be studied as a separate segment of literature if sex in itself determines a particular mode of writing, perspective, or content. In the case of Chicana writers, perspective and content have differed only to the degree that the literary work has focused on women, their sexuality, their oppression, and their creative power. Like male Chicano writers, Chicanas have dealt as well with a number of social issues and cultural themes, especially in the poetic mode. Yet, beyond thematic differences, what distinguishes Chicana writers is their relative invisibility. The greater recognition bestowed on male writers by Chicano literary critics, literature profesors, and publishers is not determined by the quality of their work; perhaps the impact of male control of Chicano publication enterprises should be considered. Few Chicano writers, male or female, are published elsewhere.

Quantitatively, then, the greater portion of production in Chicano literature has been by male writers. The smaller number of Chicana writers has been primarily in poetry, but none has gained the international or national recognition of an Alurista or an Hinojosa-Smith. The large number of women in poetry correlates directly with the large number of Chicano male poets. This genre, like that of theater, has introduced numerous creative and artistic innovations and allowed for a good deal of experimentation at both a linguistic and technical level. The greater part of our poetic production, however, is still struggling with form and constrained by the reiteration of culturalist-mythic content. Ideologically, this poetry, whether the production of Chicanos or Chicanas, has a pendular reach that encompasses purely subjectivist positions, socially oriented and critical perspectives, as well as the highly visible cultural-mythic syndrome. Technically, we have produced a number of pioneers in poetic expression at the same time that we have produced a great deal of weak poetry.

Among the pioneers are Chicana poets like Alma Villanueva, Bernice Zamora, and Lorna Dee Cervantes, who though ideologically similar to male Chicano writers, have produced esthetically superior works and dealt with various woman-related themes. The lyrical quality of these poets is often unmatched by that of major male Chicano poets. Yet, even Chicana poetry that may be structurally and artistically weak has allowed the female voice to ring out in protest against sexual abuse and victimization as well as in praise of women's resoluteness in their daily struggles against the various forces of oppression in our society.

Chicano prose production, on the other hand, whether produced by males or females, has not been at the forefront of any narrative movement. Technically, prose writers are still developing their craft; linguistically, they have not been as daring as the poets, although ideologically they reflect, for the most part, the same political perspectives. Chicano novels, specifically those written in Spanish, are often fragmented, disjointed collections of sketches or short stories, with a cultural thread tying the whole quite loosely together. There is little development of plot; characters often lack depth, and there is little concern for analyzing the major contradictions that face the Chicano population today, except at a surface or descriptive level.

These prose works often reduce the Chicano conflict to a personal crisis of identity or to a search for indigenous roots and forsaken gods. The product of higher education, Chicano writers often view themselves from the perspective of post-revolutionary Mexican essayists seeking to explain the failure and nonrevolutionary status of the revolts of 1910 in terms of an indigenous/Hispanic duality (which leads to an existential crisis, à la Octavio Paz) by situating the Chicano in a similar cultural bind: the Anglo-Mexican dichotomy. This cultural relativism permeates even the *costumbrista* sketches where the Chicano "essence" is revealed through the portrayal of colorful figures — mere shadows projected across a broad textual screen — whose lives are recounted through brief anecdotes.

Chicana prose writers have been largely ignored by Chicano critics. Mention of Chicana writers is generally limited to poets as is evident in most Chicano literature anthologies or collections, which have included at least some female writers. Even journal issues dedicated to Chicanas, like *La Palabra* (Vol. 2, No. 2, otoño 1980), are almost exclusively dedicated to the analysis of poetry or the presentation of poems (with three short prose exceptions). The same is true of *El Fuego de Aztlán*'s issue on Chicanas (Vol. 1, No. 4, Summer 1977), which offers only two prose selections but numerous poetic texts. Chicana prose writers do, however, exist. Probably the best known among them is Estela Portillo Trambley, whose stories in *Rain of Scorpions and Other Writings* (Tonatiuh International, 1974) are English renditions of short tales of death, redemption, evil, Indian gods, and nature as well as of people's strength, goodness, inner light, and search for a deeper truth about life and about themselves. The stories are thus idealistic; here the poor and oppressed find happiness in themselves and learn to accept what life metes out with a smile. The more rebellious are saved from their struggle and despair by love, by seers, or through spiritual enlightenment. The writing is a mixture of narrative discourse and dialogue from the perspective of an omniscient storyteller who sees into various hearts and minds and pauses philosophically to dwell upon a beetle's armor, a honeysuckle, a mountainside, a dusty road, a pilgrimage, or a mud flood. The flowing narrative style captures life as unchanging in essence although moving at different speeds and appearing in different hues and shades of color.

The writing of the Chicana authors to be discussed here contrasts sharply with that of Portillo Trambley. Far from being silky and nostalgic for life's simple blessings and truths, the writing of Gina Valdés and Sylvia Lizárraga is raw and gaunt, with the urgency of souls who have lived through desolation, alienation, and social contradictions themselves. The two have formed part of a group of Chicano and Latino writers in San Diego who share similar thematic interests: the social, economic, and political conditions under which Chicanos and Mexicanos live and struggle daily. These Chicana writers are particularly concerned with the problems of female workers on both sides of the border. No one denies that male writers are also capable of producing works concerned with female characters, but, unfortunately, the female characters that appear in some of our better known Chicano novels are portrayed as either naive, unfaithful, opportunistic, dumb, or supernaturally endowed. Female characters are usually part of the backdrop, the necessary background color to enable a male character to shine, suffer, or die. Chicana writers do not write exclusively about females (nor should they be expected to), but in these San Diego writers there is undoubtedly a desire to portray women as intelligent beings, capable of thought and analysis as well as feeling, and as active subjects with the capacity to act and determine the outcome of events.

Gina Valdés' novel and short stories in *There Are No Madmen Here,* although just recently published by Maize Press, was written in 1976. A poet as well as prose writer, Gina has recently completed her Masters degree in Literature at UCSD. In the following section we will look first at her novel *María Portillo* (included in the Maize collection) and comment as well on some of her other stories.

María Portillo

Like Chicana poets, the novelist Valdés works a textual braid consisting of three major narrative strands: the personal, the economic, and the cultural. Although the weaving is at times uneven, with one strand predominating at the beginning and another toward the end of the novel, all are constants in the text and are necessarily interconnected as the story threads through the social and economic struggles of Mexican immigrants in the United States, the personal plight and fortitude of a single working mother with three teenage daughters, and the cultural diversity of an extended Mexican-origin family which slowly shatters and disintegrates even as it clings to itself for survival.

The novel begins with the plight of María Portillo, abandoned by a rather bohemian husband who, in almost trendy style, takes off to Yucatán to commune with the gods and nature and to write poetry. The husband's status as a college literature professor and the stark poverty of the Portillo family in Ensenada, Baja California, set the stage for a series of contradictions to follow. Faced with starvation, María determines to break with the past — symbolically burning her wedding dress — and to return to the United States where most of her family resides and where her daughters were born before they were dragged back to Mexico by María's husband.

The personal story of María is interwoven tightly with the socio-economic narrative strand as we see her struggling to find a home for her family and work in the garment industry. The latter pays such low wages that she is forced to supplement her income with the selling of tequila smuggled across the border by her brother Ramón. The smuggling of tequila is a family affair involving brothers, sisters, and cousins; it is a family business that can be traced back to the grandfather's tequila distillery in Mexico, through the father's bootlegging period in the United States, and on up to the son's tequila smuggling.

In opposition to this modern development of the family's liquor business stands the educated grandson Valentín, who proposes dope smuggling as a more profitable venture.

The third strand outlining the Chicano family's cohesiveness and partial disintegration blends in to reveal the various relationships among members of the extended family — some positive, some destructive — and the patterns of socialization that characterize it. Central to this strand are the descriptions of Friday-night parties, family picnics, holiday celebrations, and a family outing to a Russian village across the border in Mexico. These various scenes of family unity contrast with the old-maid aunts' intolerable attitude toward the Portillo women and the family's rejection of the father, don Severino, who lives in isolation in a downtown hotel like countless other elderly and retired citizens of little means. María's fortitude and determination to survive also contrast with the destructive alcoholism of her younger brothers whose eventual deaths, like that of don Severino, bring the novel to its final episode: Ramón's arrest and trial for smuggling parrots and tequila after what was to be his last trip across the border.

The novel is thus the story of an immigrant family although it focuses on María Portillo — a strong but sketchily portrayed woman — and her daughters. As these characters make contact with relatives and friends, the reader becomes aware of the various options open to immigrants: low-wage employment, low-income housing, crime, alcoholism, institutionalization (mental hospitals and jails), education, and assimilation (one of María's daughters marries an Anglo, another goes east to study, and the third elopes to Japan with a Japanese boy). Against these options, the family offers some resistance, whether through clever subversion of the law or through cultural adaptation, while relying on the group for moral and sometimes economic support. The group's cohesiveness, on the other hand, is constantly being torn asunder by external and internal forces. The fact that the novelist has dedicated a great deal of space to the presentation of family pleasures — which come in the sharing of food, drink, and conversation — does not, however, ameliorate the overall picture of the family's daily struggle to survive in this society.

In outlining the life of an entire family through the members' interaction with the main character María, the novel has failed to deal in depth with any one specific character or problem. There are aspects of María's character that are handled quite gingerly, as if the novelist were only willing to hint at certain aspects of her relationship with her husband, the character Hernández, her father, her daughters, and her brothers. Thus, even though the female characters are central to the novel, they remain enigmas to the end. María's personal plight is secondary; this allows the novel to take another course: the story of the tequila smuggling, viewed within the context of a working-class Mexican family nucleus.

María's change from subservient wife to stalwart of the Portillo family occurs rapidly — in the first five pages of the novel — and thereafter she is unwavering in her strength. Much more vividly portrayed, on the other hand, is her father don Severino, who appears in only a few episodes and is also the main character of one of the short stories preceding the novel. Through the inclusion of rough details, the novelist captures the life of an old man in a run-down hotel in downtown Los Angeles who reads a great deal, drinks a lot of wine, does battle daily with several replicas of saints who end upside down on his little altar or under the bed when things do not go his way, and dares to complain daily to the hotel manager about a malfunctioning elevator that eventually causes the death of several lodgers. María, on the other hand, whose trek we follow throughout the novel, remains a distant character; the author does not allow her to break out of the protective mold within which she has encased her.

Short Stories

Since the writing of this novel, Gina Valdés' prose has evolved, both technically and ideologically, in character portrayal and plot development. Her more recent stories portray individuals having to grapple with concrete external forces, be they mental institutions, the church, or the school system, as well as with internal community traditions and values. Her Master's thesis is a collection of stories that evidence her interest in narrative innovation and the introduction of rhythm and verse within the narrative itself. This is the case of "Rhythms," the first story in *There Are No Madmen Here,* which reveals María's youngest daughter's alienation in a classroom through the reveries of two young Chicanas as they half-listen to the history instructor while daydreaming of the barrio dance, a mythic Indian past, and summer in Mexico with María's sister, Aunt Emilia.

Narrative experimentation and the use of various dimensions also distinguish the story "Este es un cuento," which does not appear in the Maize collection but is part of her Master's thesis. Like Cortázar's story "Las Babas del Diablo" ("Blowup"), this story is about writing — the daily grind of writing and the theory of writing. The story's first dimension is the personal account of a female writer who places creative production above socializing and often above the traditional duties assigned to the mother role. The second dimension is academia, where a lecturing university professor discuses the theory of the short story as well as varying perspectives on literature and on the ultimate objective of art. These lectures trigger further discussion by the writer-student and her classmates outside the classroom. The third dimension is the actual story that is being written by the main character. This story-within a story is a poetic narration about a female singer whose marriage is falling apart as the incurable illness of the couple's child progresses and leads to the child's death. This story, like many by Valdés, is written in Spanish and then translated into English. Those stories written bilingually, however, are not translated.

Not all of Valdés' stories focus on female characters, although all deal with life on both sides of the border. For example, one of her stories in the *Requisa 32* story collection, "El Valle del Sol," presents the theme of social oppression from the perspective of a disillusioned priest struggling with church bureaucracy as he tries to serve a number of Mexican parishioners. Another story, "There Are No Madmen Here" (which precedes the María Portillo novel) presents an episode in the life of María, now a more vividly helpless and persecuted woman than the character in the novel, that deals with the nightmare of the sane who are judged insane.

Gina Valdés is an incredibly productive writer whose style is changing as she moves from a more descriptive enumeration of anecdotes and episodes in the lives of her characters to more complex textual analyses that penetrate the characters' inner turmoil as they are flailed and swayed by external social, economic, and political forces. The more she writes, the more she develops her talents. She will undoubtedly become one of the best prose writers in Chicano literature.

The production of female writers is especially important in terms of its portrayal of women and attitudes toward women. Writing, as we all know, is conscious creative production, despite the assertions of the surrealist writers who proposed spontaneous writing. The writer, then, as subject, selects the material and tools with which he or she produces the literary work. Since the writer as subject is also socially conditioned, he or she will reveal the ideological perspectives with which he/she views the world. A writer's attitude toward women will therefore be revealed in the feminine portrayals. Feminist historians have noted that male novelists often portray women as they would like them to be—or, we might add, as they would like them to remain. For this reason, the work of female writers (especially Chicana prose writers) is important, for it offers the possibility of another view of women in literature, although this is not necessarily always the case. Female characters in the prose of Portillo Trambley, for example, are primarily presented in nurturing, passive roles, at times full of ambition that easily dissolves into evil and leads to disaster and death ("The Trees"); but they are also seen in non-conventional roles willing to defy social conventions ("The Paris Gown") to escape an unwanted marriage or, like Beatriz ("If It Weren't For the Honeysuckle . . ."), willing to end the life of a depraved man to save a young girl.

The prose of another San Diego Chicana writer, Sylvia Lizárraga, offers a unique perspective and portrayal of Chicana women. Lizárraga, now an assistant professor at UC Berkeley in the Department of Ethnic Studies and Chicano Studies, has published several short stories in the *Requisa 32* story collection. Although the major concern of the writer is the oppression of the Mexican-origin population, the main characters in her stories are primarily women: strong-willed women capable of taking action, dependent women subject to the whims of a pimp, working-class women subject to humiliation by would-be employers, defenseless women subject to rape, quick-thinking women capable of saving an undocumented worker from the grasp of the Migra (the Immigration Service patrol), and intelligent women eager to learn and receive an education at whatever age. Lizárraga's style varies from story to story. In her story of the rape, "Camino del lago," the suspense builds up rapidly from a supermarket parking lot to a deserted road where the violent scene takes place. The story, however, is more than the rape account; through a dual discourse combining a third-person narrative with a first-person account of what is occurring, the reader enters the woman's consciousness and discovers her problems, her economic constraints, her loneliness, and her limited independence. This single working mother has options, very limited options but in the end these (or the consideration of these) appear to have been left far behind; yet, they are the sole flicker of light in the distance for the victim.

Lizárraga's varied narrative style is also evident in "Quinceañera," a story about a fifteen-year-old prostitute about to give birth to her pimp's child. In this story, told from the perspecive of the young girl, there is again a constant shifting from first-person to third-person narration, a technique that allows the narrative voice to explain the girl's background and to set the scene while at the same time allowing the reader to view the world through the young girl's innocent eyes.

This juxtaposition of narrative voices creates an ironical situation, adding impact to the girl's condition and abuse. There is brief dialogue, but the major part of the text is this dual discourse that allows for a rapid shift from the girl's stream of consciousness to the bleak world that surrounds her.

Lizárraga's stories, written originally in Spanish, have been translated into English by Clara Lomas, the author's daughter Marta, and Lizárraga herself. One of her best stories does not appear in the *Requisa* volume. It is "El Don," a story about a woman's invisibility, about a woman's discovery that she is invisible to others. The story goes beyond the plight of this specific woman or women in general. It points to the psychological oppression suffered by all who are socially and economically oppressed; it crystalizes the subtle humiliation suffered by members of the working class or minorities even when they are among their so-called liberal friends. Status is the name of the game and those seen as subordinate are quietly ignored, as if they were invisible.

"El Don," has appeared in Nasario García's short story collection *Nuevos Horizontes* as well as in *Revista Chicano-Riqueña, Caracol, Metamorfosis,* and newspapers in Ensenada and Mexicali. The first-person narrative, although historically tied to a particular event in the life of the author, has become the expression of us all, those of us with the "gift" of being ignored.

The stories of Sylvia Lizárraga are short and incisive narrations combining different narrative styles and different voices (both male and female) to penetrate particular social problems and to reveal ever so lightly the inner anguish of the oppressed. Lizárraga's perspicacity and ironical tone will undoubtedly shine through many other narratives to come.

The prose of Lizárraga and Valdés touches on many of the themes found in the poetry of Chicana writers, yet the prose form allows for a broader and more in-depth analysis and projection that are necessary in Chicano literature if it is to be the artistic expression of all the Chicano population, both male and female. Existent shortcomings in prose technique and plot development have not been resolved nor can we yet be satisfied with current efforts for a necessary integration of form, content, and a progressive ideology. Chicana writers like Valdés and Lizárraga are concrete evidence that we are headed in the right direction and that Chicana women are not only important producers of Chicano intellectual and artistic work but also leaders in the forging of a progressive, highly developed cultural production. As Chicanas become more educated and more politicized, they will also become more vocal and demand the right to increased verbal expression through available print media. The importance of encouraging and stimulating women to write is obvious, but as critics we also need to consider that sex is no guarantee of progressive cognition. For this reason, we should encourage the creation of writing workshops or writers' meetings where texts can be critically analyzed, reviewed, and discussed in order to move beyond brief sketches of life in the barrio.

UNIVERSITY OF CALIFORNIA, SAN DIEGO

References

Prose

Lizárraga, Sylvia. "Camino del lago," "Quinceañera," "El regreso," "Monarquía," "Management," "El momento," and "Doña Lola." In *Requisa treinta y dos.* Ed. Rosaura Sánchez. San Diego: UCSD, Chicano Research Publications, 1979. Pp. 29-49. Translations, pp. 119-140.
Portillo Trambley, Estela. *Rain of Scorpions and Other Writings.* Berkeley: Tonatiuh International, 1975.
Valdés, Gina. *There Are No Madmen Here.* San Diego: Maize Press, 1981.
———. "El Valle del Sol." In *Requisa treinta y dos.* San Diego: UCSD, Chicano Research Publications, 1979. Pp. 59-64. Translation, pp. 147-152.

Poetry

Cervantes, Lorna Dee. *Emplumada.* Pittsburgh: University of Pittsburgh Press, 1981.
Corpi, Lucha. "Poetry Selections." In *Fireflight.* Trans. Catherine Rodríguez Nieto. Berkeley: Westcoast Print Center, 1976. Pp. 43-83.
Cota-Cárdenas, Margarita. *Noches despertando inconciencias.* Tucson: Scorpion Press, 1977.
Hernández Tovar, Inés. *Con razón corazón.* Austin: n.p., n.d.
Moreno, Dorinda. *La mujer es la tierra. La tierra da vida.* Berkeley: Westcoast Print Center, 1975.
Vigil, Evangelina. *Nade y nade.* San Antonio: M & A Editions, 1978.
Villanueva, Alma. *Bloodroot.* Austin: Place of Herons Press, 1977.
Zamora, Bernice. *Restless Serpents.* Menlo Park, CA: Diseños Literarios, 1976.

Anthologies

El Fuego de Aztlán. Issues dedicated to la Chicana. Ed. Bernice Zamora. Vol. 1, No. 4, summer 1977.
Moraga, Cherrie and Gloria Anzaldua, eds. *This Bridge Called My Back. Writings by Radical Women of Color.* Watertown, MA: Persephone Press, 1981.
La Palabra. (Tempe, Arizona). Vol. 2, No. 2, otoño 1980.

PERSONAL VISION IN
THE SHORT STORIES OF
ESTELA PORTILLO TRAMBLEY

Eliud Martínez

> This book is designed to bring the
> sexes closer together, not to set them
> apart by placing one above the other.
> If in these pages the natural superior-
> ity of women is emphasized, it is be-
> cause the fact has thus far received far
> too little attention. . . .
>
> — Ashley Montagu, *The Natural
> Superiority of Women*

In recent years, some Chicano writers have dealt increasingly in their works with larger realms of human experience, history, and knowledge. This expansion of artistic vision is reflected in the complex narrative styles, language, forms, and techniques which Chicano writers employ and which are to be found in world literature of the past and the present.[1] Consequently, contemporary Chicano literature may be said to have broken its artistic limits; challenging new directions for our present and future writers are everywhere. Chicano writers, men and women, seem to realize now that they are, as Octavio Paz would say, contemporaries of people from all over the world.

Estela Portillo Trambley is a Chicana writer who believes that Chicano literary expression should have no limits. Concerning the reading she has done that has shaped her art and personal vision, she has said:

> I read philosophy, history, psychology: Bergson, Jung, Jaspers,
> Nietzsche, Huxley, the Bible, Toynbee, Aisley. I read Buddha,
> Lao-tzu, Kahlil Gibran, Pierre Teilhard de Chardin.[2]

And as an English major she read other writers, she tells us:
T.S. Eliot, Pound, Sartre, Genet, Balzac, the Russian writers. "One
summer — she adds — I picked up Octavio Paz, and he opened the
door to Vasconcelos, López Velarde, Alfonso Reyes, Pellicer, Novo,
Pablo Neruda, and Asturias."[3]

Regarding Chicano literature, she has also made comments that
shed light on her own esthetic ideas and beliefs:

> The future of Chicano literature lies not in the de-emphasis of the
> distinctive characteristics. It will be the incorporation of still un-
> tapped, humanistic resources outside our barrio existentialism,
> mythical font, or the romantic hold on "remembrances of things
> past." It lies in a convergence of truths . . . that focus the whole
> world.[4]

Even today, there is still a critical lag among some critics of
Chicano literature in dealing with writers like Estela Portillo
Trambley, whose views and literary art challenge the more
traditional, popular barrio attitudes and assumptions regarding what
should be the nature and function of Chicano literature.[5] Consequently, despite the interest in literature by and about Chicanas that
has existed for many years, the critical bibliography on this Chicana
writer is short indeed.[6] Happily, however, one notes a greater
willingness among Chicanos to broaden their perspectives and to
understand the diversity of artistic sensibility among Chicano writers
whose experiences within the group are different in some respects and
who do not lend themselves to easy classification.

It is in this spirit, I suggest, that one must approach the short
stories of Estela Portillo Trambley in *Rain of Scorpions and Other
Stories.*[7] In style, characterization, themes, and, above all, in the
personal vision of the writer, her stories tap large realms of human
experience, intellectual history, and knowledge. Nevertheless, Estela
Portillo Trambley does deal with barrio experiences, although she
does not make them the focus of her writings.

The writer herself guides the reader toward the dominant aspect
of her personal vision. "I have a hang-up about language. I like to
say, whee, look at me, look at the beautiful words." And regarding
the art of writing, which she says does not place Chicanos or anyone
at a disadvantage, she states:

It is an instinctual and artistic pull. It is a love, an actualization. There are really no obstacles for one who loves life, people, ideas, words, and the glorious orgy of creation itself. . . . The writer who senses, intuits, and knows he is a writer achieves an autonomy inconceivable of boundaries.[8]

Personal vision emerges from a combination of elements in a work of art. Portillo Trambley mentions several whenever she speaks of her writing and of the art of writing in general. These elements include the choice and quality of language, style, vocabulary, images, tone, and symbols. A love of life, people, ideas, words, and creation itself will express that love in themes. Each element of a work of art, singly and collectively, tells the reader where the sympathies of the writer fall, toward which values he or she is inclined, and which characters best reflect the writer's way of thinking and feeling.[9]

Marcel Proust, for example, pointed out in a short essay on Goethe the importance of place, themes, and characters.[10] Underlining what he felt to be a general truth about writers, Proust stated that the topics or themes to which writers habitually recur in their books show what has fired their inspiration and what has made a strong impression on their minds. After giving a few examples from Goethe's works, the French writer states:

One feels that these things were not merely put in to please, but that they had an extremely serious bearing on his intellectual life; that the concern of his intellect was to analyze the pleasure he drew from them . . . and to ascertain their effect on the mind.

In parenthesis, Proust added that "it is by an essentially higher kind of pleasure that things important to the intellect first impose themselves on it and declare their importance."

Characters, too, according to Proust, embody a special kind of mind, see the world in a certain light, and therefore characters show the habitual preoccupations of the writer's mind. In sum, Proust asserts, "Goethe's novels cannot give us a complete statement about Goethe, but they show his preference of mind . . . plainly. . . . For it is . . . in our books that we record ourselves, our true selves."

What then, one may ask regarding Estela Portillo Trambley, do her language and style tell us about her personal outlook? What are the themes to which she habitually recurs? And what do her female and male characters tell us about this Chicana writer's mind? What are the things that fascinate her? And, finally, what do the elements that combine in the short stories tell us about the way that she thinks and feels?

The beginning and the ending of some of her stories provide good examples of her language and prose style. "Pay The Criers," for example, begins in the following way:

> Rain knows the earth and loves it well, for rain is the passion of the earth. It is tears, joy, hope, melted into cool torrents that fall on the longing and the hunger of the earth in rigorous tenderness to give her life. How well it speaks of senses in its cool excitement. The beginning of passion is a burst of flame. Its culmination speaks of an open door unto light, a lucidity of life, more life, forever life. (p. 25)

The ending of the same story starts out in the following way:

> In the atmosphere that diffuses light, there is a celestial song of currents and higher mathematics. There is the push and flux of life that finds its way to man. Man tastes it as a freedom, a way of depths, a way of new life. If the skill lies in the freedom, thought Chucho, then it belongs to death as well as life. (p. 40)

"I like to say," Portillo Trambley has told us, "whee, look at me, look at the beautiful words." These two passages show that Portillo Trambley is a writer who venerates language both for its own sake and because of its powers to dramatize ordinary phenomena—in this case, rain and copulation. Her language is eloquent, sometimes exquisite, and always correct. Her style is philosophical, at times erudite, and in many cases conceptual. In almost all her stories she includes allusions to great books and authors, to the Bible, philosophy, intellectual history, and so on. One finds very few contractions in her writings and only a sprinkling of Spanish words, which she does not force. The rhythm of her prose is lyrical, her figures of speech are evocative, the images are forceful and symbolic.

When one considers the philosophical thoughts she attributes to her character Chucho in "Pay the Criers," one is tempted to say that the characterization leaves something to be desired. One may take another view, however. For Portillo Trambley the beauty of language, the eloquence of style, the fascination with an optimistic philosophy of life—these, it seems safe to say, take precedence, in most cases, over the desire for verisimilitude of the characters or the stories. To judge her work by norms other than those that her works obey would be inappropriate.

In another story, "The Trees," we find a combination of many of these and additional prose style elements. At the beginning of this story, with a generous paragraph, Portillo Trambley describes a setting and in so doing she establishes a mood and atmosphere that are Romantic in imagery and modern in their bleakness.[11] She describes what was once a "paradise" as a "wasteland," in a way that may remind some readers of the beginning of Juan Rulfo's *Pedro Páramo* or of T.S. Eliot's *Wasteland.*

> The dead valley. Tombstones sprouted on a hill, scattered like old pennons along the valley, clustered in the shadows of a deserted house, and on the stamp of bank along a dead stream next to the hill. Dispirited, the wind moaned its own "Amen." Clusters of dry weeds hugged against the moan while rootless tumbleweeds found a path free-styled following the wind. Unpredictable, these jumbled skeletons of brush found refuge against tree stumps, doorways, and tombstones. (p. 11)

In the continuation of this first paragraph the intellectual side of the writer becomes noteworthy. The narrator of the story begins to ponder and to ask philosophical questions about death, nothingness, time, human error, the processes of human life. The tone of the writing is still Romantic, and the philosophical questions are expressed poetically, symbolically, and mystically:

> Even dead valleys cling to traces of something. This something is new because it is now in the instance of process.

And:

> All is part of the change in process, errant and eternal. The reality now is different from the reality then . . . a life emerged, then, a desolation in the duration we call time.

In these passages the Romantic sensibility and the intellectual side of the writer are blended. To these is added now that side of the writer which is the social commentator:

> But things and people of the earth are creation and self-created by complexities beyond comprehension. That is why blame and condemnation of people should not exist, for they are but creations of a process, self-created with ingredients from creations outside themselves. This valley thrived once; so did its people, following patterns known and unknown.

Despite the writer's statements regarding the undesirability of social commentary in artistic expression, it is to be found generously in her stories, and not only in the feminist quality of her work.[12] In the social commentary of the last part of this paragraph the narrator is telling us something significant by addressing what one may call eternal and timeless verities, generalities about time and change and about nameless people who follow patterns of life that are known and unknown. What is the narrator saying? The social commentary is not completely subordinated to the lyrical prose style, language, and imagery. The author is making — via the narrator — a conceptual statement. Perhaps it is up to the reader to discern it.

Is it too farfetched to speculate about the author's symbolic statement? Can this dead valley be a symbol of all the dead "valleys" where great and ancient civilizations once flourished and attained world renown? Is it farfetched to think of the rise and fall of great nations and empires, of conquerors and conquered? Can the valley of "The Apples" be a symbol of the Valley of Mexico at the time of the Conquest, a symbol of the great pre-Columbian empire razed by the Spaniards?

The principle that the author expresses through the narrator — that blame and condemnation of people should not exist — is really timeless and eternal. In a statement coming from a writer who knows the work of Octavio Paz, Vasconcelos, and Alfonso Reyes, a Chicana writer who has lamented an excess of complaint and condemnation in Chicano literature and the polarization between Chicano culture and American culture, it does not seem out of place to ponder whether she has not made a social statement about the Mexican heritage which is consistent with her views, whether she makes it consciously or unconsciously, or perhaps intuitively.[13]

"The Trees" shares many of the prose style qualities of the other stories. In addition, it reminds one of the Mexican corrido tradition.[14] One aspect of the story is about two brothers, Rafael and Ismael, and the jealousy of the latter, who is deceived by his wife Nina into believing that she has been raped by Rafael. Nina, the female protagonist of the story, actually seduces her brother-in-law Rafael:

> Afterwards, Rafael felt a remorse. The fabric of brothers' trust had been violated. He dared not think of what had happened. . . . Nina was amused by his total suffering. She felt him to be a hypocrite. Just like a man. . . . All of them were Pontius Pilates. (p. 15)

To increase his torment and remorse, she informs him that she will tell.

Rafael was one of four drunken men, the reader learns, who had violated Nina many years before (p. 19). In order to avenge herself she makes her husband believe that she has been raped. Deceived by Nina, Ismael sets out to kill his brother. When Ismael is about to shoot Rafael, he accidentally kills his other brother Marcos, who in trying to prevent the killing gets in the line of fire (p. 21).

The suspense that had built up after Nina's seduction of Rafael and a chain of misfortunes that attend Nina's "rape" are described in a manner that reminds one of Greek tragedy:

> The town now spoke of the growing curse. Trees were dying; workers were leaving the Ayala orchards. The assailant of Ismael's wife had not been found. Santos had died of a heart attack trying to save his wife who died in the fire. Nina was said to be going insane. Rafael was a broken drunk. Ismael was obsessed with the idea of revenge. Marcos was trying hopelessly to save the vestiges of family. Hubris, catastrophic pride . . . avenging furies on the heads of the town's nobility . . . fruit . . . all melting into a great velocity of madness. (pp. 19-20)

The story also contains allusions to the Bible. Nina is described as "an Eve in a Garden of Eden" and "she was also the snake" (p. 13) and the apple:

> Nina was like the Quinteca apple . . . soft, with that special sweetness . . . with that sensuality that spells life . . . she was so special . . . so exciting. Nina was the Quinteca apple in the moonlight. (p. 15)

After Ismael has accidentally killed his brother Marcos, Nina looks down from the top of the hill to which she has fled from Rafael. Below her, from a height that emphasizes her woman's power over the Ayala brothers, she contemplates the scene of the grief-stricken Ismael placing his dead brother's body on the ground. "She looked down at Cain standing over the body of Abel" (p. 21).

In the valley to which Nina came after she married Ismael, "men and women had a separate given image until Nina came" (p. 13). She brought to this paradise a wrath that was shaped by a loveless childhood and by the four men who violated her (pp. 17-19). Nina plotted against men, her oppressors, and she won. Or did she? She used the special sweetness of her sensuality—that sensuality which spells life—as a strength to destroy. It was a dubious strength, in a sense, because it was nourished by fear and lovelessness and by the absence of freedom.

The depiction of Nina is eloquent and compassionate (p. 13). At the end of the story Eve and all women are exonerated from the easy blame cast upon them by men because of their sex. The feminist social commentary is inescapably obvious; its tone of compassion for women's plight appeals to the emotions.

Just before Nina plunges to her death, she remembers the sweetness after the dark, screaming battles of the spirit. She remembers when Ismael came into her life:

> He had loved her with a gentle touch. But how could she love? She
> did not know how. . . . Sooner or later death comes. He had said
> many things which she did not understand because he had never
> known light and freedom. . . . All the beautiful things I am . . . the
> confidence, the power . . . one large, frightened sob? . . . Nina
> called out, "God, are you there?" (p. 22)

In the depiction of Nina's death the Romantic sensibility of the author
is most evident:

> She leaned over simply to be caught by wind and the openness of
> things. A shower of rocks followed the path of her falling body in full
> symphony. It sang the praises of something new in erosive change.
> Not a nothingness, but a coming desolation. When her body hit the
> bottom of the hill, the praises followed like the lingering fullness of
> one note until her body was covered with debris. She was now part
> of all. . . . (p. 22)

The preceding examples of Estela Portillo Trambley's literary art
have demonstrated that she is a writer of Romantic sensibility, a
philosophical thinker, and a social commentator. Many other passages from her stories, as we shall see, exemplify the first of these
characteristics, and in them one can identify several general and
related traits of the Romantic sensibility.[15]

First of all, writers of Romantic sensibility recognize the importance of imagination in works of art. Imaginative art is not bound
by the rules and norms of literary verisimilitude.

Romantic writers love to describe landscape scenes of forests,
woods, mountains, desolate and solitary places, graveyards; they are
fascinated with the silence and stillness of night. They are drawn to
wild, untamed, and melancholy aspects of nature and to scenes that
strike the eye and arouse the emotions of whoever contemplates them,
including the reader. They often stress a correspondence between
nature and character and between nature and states of the soul.

Writers of Romantic sensibility often emphasize magical,
mystical, legendary, and epic qualities of setting, atmosphere, and
character, qualities which appeal to the spirit, emotions, and senses.
Consequently, they describe objects, events, and characters subjec-
tively in order to emphasize reactions to them and the effects that they
produce in the writer, the observer, and the reader.

Romantic writers are fascinated with remembrances, history, and
things of the past; with things that are remote, dead, unknown, old,
mythical, or legendary; and with mystical, inexplicable, and "in-
expressible" states of mind.

In terms of artistic expression, writers of Romantic sensibility favor poetic images, lyrical language, and suggestive figures of speech. They use a tone that expresses many kinds of responses to human experience: a sense of loss, regret, melancholy; a veneration for life and nature; a lament about all that diminishes our goodness and humanity; a sense of the ephemeral quality of life.

But Romantic writers also recognize "that everything in creation is not humanly *beautiful,* that the ugly exists beside the beautiful, the unshapely beside the graceful, the grotesque on the reverse of the sublime, evil with good, darkness with light."[16] In literature that is Romantic, consequently, every conceivable kind of human being may be depicted. The writer of Romantic sensibility, however, gravitates toward characters who are dreamers, solitaries, visionaries; they are frequently introspective, sensitive, passionate, moody, inquisitive, and imaginative.[17] Other characters, such as those one finds in some stories of Portillo Trambley, are usually free spirits. They express the author's love of freedom of every sort.

Even though Portillo Trambley is a writer of Romantic sensibility, the intellectual side of the writer is most prominent. Her stories are characterized by a love of ideas and a fascination with intellectual order, conceptual systems, life patterns, and reason. One notes in the stories that she classifies and interprets ideas and patterns of order in human life. Her characters discuss issues and debate ideas. She is a writer who loves books, the life of the mind, and human knowledge. The topics to which she habitually recurs and the intellectual realms of knowledge on which she draws include art, philosophy, history, cultural differences and taboos, and men's oppression of women, among others.

Two stories, "If It Weren't For the Honeysuckle . . ." and "The Paris Gown," illustrate more emphatically than the others how the Romantic, the intellectual, and the social commentator blend to express Portillo Trambley's feminist outlook. In "If It Weren't For the Honeysuckle . . ." the intellectual love of order is expressed in lyrical terms:

> It had rained for three days and nights. The greenness now had a sweet heaviness. She looked up to watch the cloud movement with its secret of raindrops. The tapestry of the earth she knew well and loved because she saw an order. She loved order above all things.
> (p. 98)

But the order which Beatriz contemplates about her and which she loves is robbed of its perfection and disfigured by the presence of a man. Robles, the man, oppresses Beatriz and the other two women who live with her, Lucretia and Sofa. Robles is depicted as a man of filthy ways who is violent and cruel. He gets drunk, kicks and breaks furniture, beats Sofa and breaks her hip, and kills the cat that Beatriz has bought for Sofa (p. 101). Finally, Beatriz can no longer tolerate his cruelty.

"Beatriz felt an anger. Woman . . . the victim. . . . Why? It had no order" (p. 105). She develops a plan to poison Robles; "fungus of the world, thought Beatriz. He was old and he was meanness, but Beatriz felt no fear. He was a swollen poison with an evil smell" (p. 106).

Beatriz is one of Portillo Trambley's strong-willed women who plot actively against cruel and violent men. Her thoughts emphasize the feminist theme of freedom from the oppression of men and their values. The author expresses these angry thoughts in language that is conceptual; here, the intellectual and the social commentator overshadow the writer of Romantic sensibility:

> It had been decreed long ago by man-made laws that living things were not equal. It had been decreed that women should be possessions, slaves, pawns in the hands of men with ways of beasts. It had been decreed that women were to be walloped effigies to burn upon the altars of men. It had been decreed by the superiority of brute strength that women should be no more than durable spectacles to prove a fearful potency that was a shudder and a blow. It had been decreed . . . how long ago? . . . that women should approve of a manhood that simply wasn't there . . . the subservient female loneliness. . . . It had been decreed. (p. 106)

The repetition of the phrase "it had been decreed" underlines the ageless, monotonous oppression of women and their voiceless helplessness in the world of men, against which Beatriz rebels. In this paragraph the reader is given a symbolic portrait of Robles — man the oppressor of woman — and all men like him.

The symbolic portrait of Robles and the intolerable pattern of women's lives as "decreed" by men justify Beatriz' anger and the three women's irrevocable decision to free themselves of Robles' violent and irrational disruption of the order they need and desire in their lives. Hatred is an important theme in this and other stories (pp. 42, 94).

Another strong-willed woman character is Clotilde Romero de Traske of "The Paris Gown." Perhaps it will not be thought farfetched to suggest that her name may be symbolic of the aristocratic "blind tradition" into which she was born and which roused in her an "indignant feeling of injustice," of being "like a victim from an early age" (p. 4). According to the *Nuevo Pequeño Larousse Ilustrado* (1951 ed.),

Santa Clotilde, who died at Tours in 545 (the daughter of Gondebaldo, a king of Burgundy, and wife of Clodoveo I, a Merovingian king) brought about her husband's conversion to Christianity. Hence, the importance of the first name of the protagonist of "The Paris Gown," who rebels against the "single fate for the gentlewoman . . . one variation of the cloister or another" (p. 4); like her namesake, she is a woman who is capable of exercising influence on men. Ironically, she rebels against the stereotyped image that her name suggests.

If Romero is the paternal maiden name of the Clotilde of this story, it is doubly ironic, for it means pilgrim, one who makes pilgrimages; in other words, one who travels, which she was forbidden to do by her father because she was a woman. The last name, de Traske, suggests aristocratic social class, but it also implies that woman is the possession of the husband. However, since the protagonist of "The Paris Gown" has had numerous marriages (p. 1), it too is ironic. Further speculation about he name is unnecessary.

Like Nina of "The Trees" and Beatriz of "Honeysuckle," Clotilde Romero de Traske, as a young woman, must also plot against the barbarism of men, in this case that of her own father. Her father, she tells Theresa, had wanted to marry her off to a wealthy man who was old enough to be her father and who repulsed her. If she refused, her father threatened to send her to the cloister. The father was very unhappy with his daughter because she had "felt the gypsy spirit," because she wanted to go to Paris, because she loved laughter and art and travel, and because she competed with her brother and surpassed him in riding horses and in other activities.

Clotilde develops a plan (pp. 6-8) to outwit her domineering father, whose interest is not in his daughter but in the marriage contract to the wealthiest man around (p. 6). Her plan succeeds (pp. 8-9), to the embarrassment of her father, and to protect his reputation he sends Clotilde to Paris, which was precisely what she wanted.

Again, the portrait of Clotilde in "The Paris Gown" is alternately Romantic and intellectual, and it too expresses the feminist ideas of the author. At the beginning of the story, the author depicts Clotilde as an aristocratic woman. She is described as sophisticated, chic, existentially fluent. She is graceful and youthful, confident, flexible of body, and of a quick and discerning mind.

Then her Romantic traits are given. In Paris she is an art dealer, but she is a legend back home. She is a totally free spirit and the stories about her many marriages, her travels, her artistic ventures, and her famous friends all make her stand out in stark contrast to the women of her time. "Her life abroad had become scandal in epic to the clan of women in aristocratic circles back home" (p. 1).

Another depiction, however, seems more than a little overworked in language and imagery. Consequently, it clashes with the previously Romantic depiction of Clotilde. It is less successful than the symbolic portrait of Robles:

> Theresa was somewhat startled by the impression Clotilde made with the room as background. A convex reflection of mood, the older woman was a human focal point against the subjectivity of artistic experience in meaningful arrangement around the room. Emotionally coded, Clotilde stood, a liberated form from civilized order. All this was a sensing to Theresa who knew little about art. (p. 2)

The passage speaks for itself without commentary. It illustrates how prominent the intellectual side of her writing is.

In the three stories, "The Trees," "If It Weren't For the Honeysuckle . . ." and "The Paris Gown," the women protagonists seek revenge, and they develop plans to rebel against male-dominated traditions and values that oppress women. Their revolt and their actions are justified on emotional and intellectual terms. The characters of Romantic sensibility appeal emotionally to the reader, and the narrator justifies their revolts intellectually.

In "The Paris Gown" the intellectual side of Estela Portillo Trambley and her feminist ideas are more prominent than in the other stories. This story contains sections that approximate brief intellectual treatises or essays. In the narrator's commentaries and in the dialogue between Clotilde and her granddaughter Theresa, a number of topics are discussed; among them are the older woman's fascination with travel and its importance in life, the relation of art and life, the conflict between barbarism and civilization in history, the blindness and barbarism of men and their violence toward women, the stifling effects of marriage on Clotilde (i.e., on women), man's use of marriage as a means to control women and keep them in "their place," the unequal treatment of women and the unfair expectations of them as contrasted with the treatment and expectations of male siblings in childhood, and male oppression as the cause of women's desire for revenge (pp. 1-5).

The theme of freedom, as one can see from the preceding and other examples, is a dominant one in the stories of Portillo Trambley —freedom for women and men. In the author's view, as Clotilde expresses it, men are also victims when women are oppressed and denied equality with men:

> ". . . I know that the instinct that respects all life, the instinct that understands equality, survives in all of us in spite of overwhelming, unfair tradition. Men know this instinct, too, although thousands of years of conditioning made them blind to the equality of all life. The violence of man against woman is a traditional blindness whose wall can be broken. Isn't that the object of love . . . to break walls?" (p. 3)

Clotilde's defiance of her father, she says, "was a kind of insanity finding its own method to fight what I considered a slavery" (p. 8). And at the end of the story when her granddaughter asks her if her life in Paris causes her to miss Mexico, the other home, Clotilde responds:

> "Yes, I left part of myself there and the people of my blood . . . of course there is a certain nostalgia . . . but no regrets. That's what I hope you will learn in your journeys . . . never to have regrets."
> "You have found . . . the freedom . . . the equality?"
> "Yes, my child, I have known the depth of feeling in all its glorious aspects." Both women looked out the window and caught the full colors of life. (p. 9)

Other characters express the same veneration for the principles of freedom and equality.

Chucho, the male character of "Pay the Criers," ponders the principle of freedom:

> One time he had seen some ice-skaters in the city. He had watched their graceful, skillful skating with great wonderment. Such a difficult thing looked so easy, so effortless. That was beauty. Somehow he felt it had something to do with the freedom he loved so well, but he could not explain it. (p. 29)

And Triano, the gypsy knife-sharpener of "Duende," embodies freedom in the way that he earns his livelihood:

> Triano loved his work. Its monetary reward was a pittance, but the days were rich with common sharing. The adventure of faces, the roar of dreams and fears, the many colors of sorrow and joy, all were a richness, a belief.
> Everyone knew the gypsy. . . . He mended things and people. He was full of the duende spirit from the mountains of the old country where survival was a precipice giving the gift of sky and barren earth. (p. 56)

Moreover, the romantic gypsy loves the night. Night represents the freedom that comes from dreams and hopes: "The night would play with dreams and hope would blossom magnificently" (p. 59). At night, Triano must be around people; "he had to drink with friends and listen to dreams. . . . The night is the total of the day; it is necessary for the full creation" (p. 67). And Fito, the Vietnam veteran of "Rain of Scorpions," also exclaims, "I . . . I want to be free . . . I don't know how to be free" (p. 126).

Estela Portillo Trambley's characters tell the reader a great deal about her personal vision. Like the language of her prose style, the characters tell us that she is fascinated with life and people of different social classes, backgrounds, cultures, and nationalities. A poetic writer, she gravitates toward Romantic, intellectual, and international types.

Characters like Clotilde (a Mexican who lives in Paris) and Julius Otto Vass Schleifer (a German who lives in Mexico) of "The Secret Room" are of aristocratic background. Characters like Clotilde, the gypsies of "Duende," the children of "Rain of Scorpions," and Nan of "Pilgrimage" express the author's interest in travel. Some of her characters are cultured and elegant people who sip wine or brandy and engage in esthetic and philosophical discussions. Portillo Trambley is fascinated with characters, as has been noted, who express a love of freedom and equality, independence and broadmindedness of thought and purpose, and others who love song and the night, who have known sorrow and joy, tragedy and vision (pp. 27, 35, 36, 67). In addition to her strong-willed women, one also finds in her stories characters who love books, who are artists, actors and actresses, gypsies, people from Chicano barrios, Vietnam veterans, and adolescent girls, among others. It is not possible in this essay to do justice to all of them.

A few additional comments, however, can be made about characterization in Portillo Trambley's stories. Her art of character depiction is varied. Some of her portraits are brief and lyrical. Others are intellectually rendered, such as the one of Clotilde. Portillo Trambley develops her characters with dialogue, figurative descriptions, and literary allusions, or by presenting the reader with their unspoken thoughts. Some of her characters, such as the American Nan of "Pilgrimage" and the German Julius of "The Secret Room," undergo a cultural metamorphosis. These two characters find in Mexico a new meaning in life, Nan when she accompanies her Mexican servant Cuca on a pilgrimage to the Basílica de Guadalupe, and Julio (as he modifies his German name) by living among the Mexican people who toil and love the earth.

> Nan became very much aware of a strange metamorphosis of spirit
> that had begun when she had crossed the border and recognized the
> freedom. Freedom? Freedom from what? Nan could not yet
> tell. . . . But she was shedding old, sad, frightening things. It was a
> new perception with sun, wind, and desert yet unclear except in
> sense. (p. 47)

The freedom, it turns out, is a freedom from hatred and rage, a
freedom to love and to know joy (pp. 42-43, 49, 53).

In "The Secret Room" Julio sheds (along with his German name)
the ideas and notions of the Germans as the master Aryan race. He
goes over in his mind the Icelandic legends of Nordic grandeur, the
memories of Germany during Hitler's rise, and his father's and his
German girlfriend's impassioned nationalism. "Germany and the
Germans are the superior race," says Helga. She is unhappy with
Julio because he does not share her views:

> Helga pouted. "You're not a good German, Julius." Julio silently
> agreed. He was not a good German. He didn't know what he was.
> (p. 82)

Julio is a Mexican citizen of German birth. He lives among the
people of Mexico. He falls in love with one of the inhabitants, Elsa,
from whom he decides to take lessons on how to see (p. 88):

> Julio took off his shirt and shoes. Then he lighted a cigarette. He
> wore the pantalones of the peon. His brown skin glistened. The
> moustache was the same as many of those worn by the farm people.
> He had become of the earth by choice. (p. 81)

Julio refuses the slavery of power. He purges the dark secret room of
his father's master race symbols. He opens the shutters, symbolically,
and lets in the light.

> There! The sun was something else. It sang about the earth, its
> constancy and neverending creations. Julio felt very, very Mexican.
> The earth people could more easily find a freedom. . . . It is the
> masters who wear the chains from within. . . . (p. 87)

These two characters, Nan and Julio, find in Mexico a freedom from
hatred, liberation from cultural biases, and spiritual happiness.

Conflicting cultural values and hatred (pp. 89-90) are also central
themes of "The Burning." In this story the extraordinary portrait of
the aged Lela, a Tarahumara *curandera*, emerges from the perceptions
of the women of the barrio and from her own memories of childhood
as she is dying in her hut. This story exemplifies the author's story-
telling gifts at their best. Many of the fine qualities of her writing that
have already been noted are to be found in this story: a Romantic

love of nature and spiritual mysticism, lyrical language, dreamlike atmosphere, and a fascination with the main character's miraculous powers of healing and her cultural belief in an afterlife (pp. 91-94).

In this story the author has made use of her knowledge of Eastern mystical philosophy, cultural anthropology, and religious superstition to write a fine Romantic story. The character portrait of Lela is epic and legendary (Ibid.).

The hate-filled women of the barrio think of Lela as a witch. They sit in council and decide to burn her hut (pp. 89-90). In the women's culture, death by fire is for sinners, heretics, and evil people. They do not know that in Tarahumara culture death by fire is the desired form of dying for those who love, who hold life and death in reverence, and who find communion in nature. While the women plot, the dying Lela prays that she may die by fire. Unaware that in Tarahumara culture fire allows the dead person to pass into Oneness with all things and to join the ancestors, the women set fire to Lela's hut. Lela's prayer is answered (pp. 95-96). The social commentary of the author is expressed by the irony.

In the depiction of Lela and other characters one is struck by their archetypal dimensions and by the lyrical language of the writer. This is true of female characters such as Refugio of "Pay the Criers," Mama Tante and Marusha of "Duende," and Lupe of "Rain of Scorpions," among others. It is also true of male characters such as Manolo and El Soldado from the story "Recast."

Estela Portillo Trambley links her characters with vital natural forces, human instinct, blood ties, myth and legend, ancestral memories, and secret, timeless psychological dramas. Two examples will suffice to illustrate further these qualities of the author's method of characterizaton. Here is a lyrical portrait of Refugio:

> In life, Refugio had been a lusty warrior full of battle cry. . . . This was her kind of grandeur. . . . She was earth with its tenacity, its instinctual freedom, and its voracity. The roughness of Refugio gave way only to a simple faith, a childish belief in the ritual wonders of her church. Its pageantry made her one with God, the master in the center of the ring. She had wanted a warrior's funeral. . . . A fiery rocket must streak the heavens. . . . A feast in her honor where tears would be wept in ceremonious grace. This had been the wish of the dead woman on the cot. (p. 27)

The author's portrait of Manolo in "Recast" is archetypal also. It is less lyrical and again the language illustrates the author's intellectual side. The story begins with a brief but panoramic anthropological survey of life since it came out of the sea. The survey then focuses on the growth of armor among some living things to protect their soft body parts. The author establishes a symbolic relationship between the armor of a dung beetle and the "armor" of human beings, in this case, her character Manolo. The following passage from the story is just a small part of the author's lengthy analogy between the dung beetle and the character:

> Manolo found only fear in loneliness. He built a beetle's armor. The interplay of his life was similar to that of beetles found under rocks. When disturbed by the removal of the rock under which they live, they eject a drop of volatile fluid from the anus, an audible explosion in a jet of smoke, acidic, caustic, destructive. Manolo had built a shell that was the emblem of . . . a heroic, handsome image. . . . (p. 70)

These kinds of connections between characters and historical pageantry (Refugio) on the one hand, and with biological evolution (Manolo) on the other, enhance the literary depictions of the characters. Ordinary human experiences such as the death of Refugio or the self-defensiveness of Manolo are dramatized. Other ordinary experiences such as sexual awakening or making love are endowed by the author with poetic sacredness.

In summary, one can say that the combination of elements in the short stories of Estela Portillo Trambley expresses a distinct personal vision in which the Romantic sensibility is dominant. This vision is inspired and erudite, poetic and intellectual, lyrical and conceptual. The variety of characters demonstrates that Portillo Trambley seeks a knowledge and understanding of peoples and cultures from all over the world, from many times in history. Even though she expresses a feminist outlook, her sympathies are toward characters, both female and male, who venerate life, joyfulness, gentleness, freedom, and equality. Some of her characters are international, but the barrio and *lo mexicano* are well represented. Some of the characters show the writer to be a social commentator.

Portillo Trambley venerates beautiful words and evocative language, the world of books. She uses language and symbols and knowledge to show the sacredness of life, its pageantry, and the time-lessness of human experience. Her words, Anaïs Nin would say, expand our human dimensions, because Portillo Trambley sees the emotional and spiritual, the mythical and legendary meaning and dimensions of human acts. There is symbolism in everything we do, says Nin.[18]

Finally, it is gratifying to see in recent years that Chicano writers and scholars recognize the limitless dimensions of Chicano literary art. Chicano writers who deserve more critical attention than they have received so far include Estela Portillo Trambley, Orlando Romero, and Nash Candelaria, who are less well known than Ron Arias, Rodolfo Anaya, Alejandro Morales, and others. An author like Portillo Trambley rightly reminds us that for Chicano writers there are still untapped humanistic resources that focus the whole world. Her work stands as a commendable example of how writers have always used the past and made it present. It reminds us that writers have always known how to use intellectual history, literature and the arts, human knowledge, myth, legend, traditions of the past and the present, and many varieties of human experience—all of that, in order to artistically express the general and the particular. One of her characters in particular, Lupe from "Rain of Scorpions," tells us much about this Chicana writer and allows the author to summarize her personal vision:

> Fito admired the fact that she had read so many books and had educated herself beyond anyone he knew in the barrio. Not with schooling, although she graduated from high school. What Fito saw in her as a form of education . . . was a kind of madness. The reading of too many books had grown into a madness, and that madness had grown wings. These wings took her to . . . libraries, museums, and free concerts by herself. . . . She had the wings of a searcher. . . . She went to look, listen, and read about eternities and the wonder of human beings. Everybody thought she was strange. She knew she was strange and was glad of it. What came, what passed, what ended, her madness shoved aside. What she kept was an eternal pulse with the greatness of things. (pp. 127-28)

UNIVERSITY OF CALIFORNIA, RIVERSIDE

Notes

This essay and others on contemporary Chicano literature have been partly supported by intramural grants. I am grateful to the Academic Senate Committee on Research at UCR for these grants.

[1] Eliud Martínez, "Contemporary Chicano Literature, II: International Literary Relations and Influences," unpublished ms. A short version of this essay was presented at the 1978 MLA Convention in San Francisco.

[2] Juan Bruce-Novoa, *Chicano Authors: Inquiry by Interview* (Austin: UT Press, 1980), p.180. Hereafter, this work will be cited as *Chicano Authors.*

³*Ibid.*

⁴*Ibid.*, pp. 180-81.

⁵The issue is not so heatedly debated as it used to be. The polemical conception of what should be the nature and function of contemporary Chicano literature is expressed very well in many parts of Luis Valdez and Stan Steiner, eds., *Aztlán: Anthology of Mexican American Literature* (New York: Vintage Books, 1972). See especially the essays in Chapter XI by Manuel J. Martínez, pp. 349-53, and Luis Valdez, pp. 354-61; the latter's "Introduction: La Plebe," pp. xiv-xxxlv and pp. 405-06. See also Francisco Jiménez, ed., *The Identification and Analysis of Chicano Literature* (New York: Bilingual Press/Editorial Bilingüe, 1979), and Elind Martínez, "*I Am Joaquín* As Poem and Film," *Journal of Popular Culture*, Vol. XIII, 3 (Winter 1979), pp. 505-15.

Ernestina Eger's excellent *A Bibliography of Criticism of Contemporary Chicano Literature* (Berkeley: UC, Chicano Studies Library Publications, 1982) provides a broad, sensible definition of Chicano literature, pp. xiii-xxi. The bibliography is truly admirable in many respects and it will shape the future of Chicano literary scholarship and facilitate investigation immeasurably.

⁶Ernestina Eger, pp. 50-51. See especially Judy Salinas, "The Role of Women In Chicano Literature," in Francisco Jiménez, ed., *op. cit.*, pp. 191-240.

⁷All citations and page references to this work are to the first printing (Berkeley: Tonatiuh International, 1975), and they will be included in parenthesis in the body of the text.

⁸*Chicano Authors*, p. 178.

⁹Some of these statements are paraphrased from Ireneo Martin Duque and Marino Fernández Cuesta, *Géneros literarios* (Madrid: Colección Plaza Mayor, 1973), pp. 173-78.

¹⁰Proust's essay is very short. The citations are from "Goethe," in Sylvia Townsend Warner, trans., *Marcel Proust: On Art and Literature, 1896-1919* (New York: Delta Books, 1958), pp. 363-66.

¹¹In all subsequent references to the Romantic sensibility of Portillo Trambley I am following the wise advice of Mario Praz, who cautions literary scholars against using literary terms too rigidly. Terms like "romantic" and "classic," he says, are "approximate terms . . . and what they cannot give — exact and cogent definition of thought — is not demanded of them." See his "Introduction: 'Romantic'; An Approximate Term," in *The Romantic Agony* (New York: Meridian Books, 1960), pp. vii-xvi.

I am also following Praz's example in leaving the reader to form his own judgment of the works from the exposition of this essay. Consequently, I have quoted generously from the short stories rather than make sweeping general interpretations that the reader would have to accept on faith. A statement regarding the sense in which I use the term "Romantic" is found in note 15, below.

¹²See her statements in the interview in *Chicano Authors*, pp. 172-75, 179-81. The first five chapters of "Rain of Scorpions," pp. 111-32, make an inventory of grievances against those who control the life and are responsible for the terrible living conditions in the "stinking hole of Smeltertown." See also pp. 72-75 of the story "Recast" for a depiction of the Chicano movement and the barrio.

¹³*Ibid.* Those interested in pursuing this polemical principle further as it concerns the Spanish-Mediterranean heritage of Mexicans may consult the following: Manuel Gamio, "España y los españoles," in *Forjando patria* (México: Editorial Porrúa, 1960), pp. 153-57; Octavio Paz, "Los hijos de la Malinche," in *El laberinto de la soledad* (México: FCE, 1959), pp. 59-80; Martín Luis Guzmán, "El verdadero concepto de la hispanidad," in *Segunda Antología* (private printing, 1969), pp. 371-76, a scathing

chastisement of José Vasconcelos; Alfonso Reyes, "México en una nuez," in *La Semana de Bellas Artes*, INBA, No. 193, 12 de agosto de 1981, pp. 9-12; and Philip Wayne Powell, *Tree of Hate* (New York: Basic Books, 1971).

Of additional benefit is a reading of Américo Castro's "Prólogo: Españolidad y europeización del *Quijote*," Miguel de Cervantes, *El ingenioso hidalgo don Quijote de la Mancha* (México: Ed. Porrúa, S.A., 1960), pp. vii-lix.

[14]See Américo Paredes, "The Folk Base of Chicano Literature," in Joseph Sommers and Tomás Ybarra-Frausto, eds., *Modern Chicano Writers* (Englewood Cliffs, N.J.: Prentice-Hall, Inc., 1979), pp. 4-17. This essay points out a "romantic point of view [that] deals not with living things but with idealization of them, in a world where there are no contemporary problems" (p. 16). From a modern perspective, "Romantic" literature seems "melodramatic" and "idealized." Contemporary writers of Romantic sensibility run the risk of being perceived unfavorably.

[15]The following traits are paraphrased from Mario Praz, *op. cit.*, who follows the historical evolution of the word which, according to Praz, Logan Pearsall Smith lucidly traced. The best essay on the subject, in my opinion, is "Romanticism" in the *Princeton Encyclopedia of Poetry and Poetics* (Princeton, N.J.: Princeton Univ. Press, 1965), pp. 717-22. This work indicates that there are 11,396 definitions of Romanticism. See also the essays on "Decadence," pp. 185-86, "Symbolism," pp. 836-39, and "Surrealism," pp. 821-23.

A very useful work that brings together many theoretical manifestos and esthetic statements regarding several European literary movements is Eugen Weber, ed., *Paths to the Present* (New York: Dodd, Mead & Co., Inc., 1970); see esp. the "Introduction," pp. 3-11, and the editor's prefatory comments to Chapter I, "Romanticism," pp. 13-17. The documents of Romanticism continue to p. 124.

Three other works, out of many, may be cited; they establish continuity between the Romanticism of the 19th century (and its persistence) and the Modernism of the 20th century: Jacques Barzun, *Romanticism and the Modern Ego* (Boston: Little, Brown and Co., 1943), Henri Peyre, *What Is Romanticism?* (University, Ala.: Univ. of Alabama Press, 1977), and Ralph Freeman, *The Lyrical Novel* (Princeton: Princeton Univ. Press, 1963). The first two chapters of Freedman's work are excellent and pertinent to this essay: "Nature and Forms of the Lyrical Novel," pp. 1-17, and "The Lyrical Tradition," pp. 18-41.

[16]Emile Zola, "Preface to Cromwell," in Eugen Weber, *op. cit.*, p. 42.

[17]Ralph Freedman, *op. cit.*

[18]Anaïs Nin. *The Novel of the Future* (New York: Collier Books, 1976). Regarding Nin's discussion of literary symbols and their relation to dreams, see pp. 12-16. Regarding symbols and the language of poetic prose, see pp. 40-43.

II. Poetry

WALKING THE THIN LINE:
HUMOR IN CHICANA LITERATURE

Tey Diana Rebolledo

> "All the most lively and sensitive children of our century are stricken by a disease unknown to doctors and psychiatrists. It is related to the disorders of the soul and might be called 'irony.' Its symptoms are fits of an exhausting laughter which starts with a diabolical mockery and a provocative smile and ends as rebellion and sacrilege."
>
> —Alexander Blok, 1908[1]

The humor of women, whether in the form of jokes, puns, satire, witticisms or other forms, has neither been carefully collected nor studied.[2] Carol Mitchell has studied female joke telling and the hostility towards males she perceives in it. Researchers have studied sex differences in the telling and appreciation of jokes.[3] Nevertheless, women's humor as *social process* has not been studied analytically. And if the material on women's humor in America is scarce, it is practically nonexistent for minority women.[4]

The purpose of this study is twofold. First, it seeks to explore some possible explanations for the scarcity of material on women's humor, and second, it proposes to analyze the particular content and possible significance of those incidents of humor found in the Chicana writers of the 1970s and 1980s.

One reason women are not perceived as joke tellers is that a large percentage of jokes are ones in which the woman is the victim. Many jokes, verbal dueling, and joking relationships are expressed in sexual terms. Among many cultures these dirty jokes and verbal dueling express a derogatory attitude toward women, who are seen as being powerless, passive, and wanton.[5] In Latin cultures, as well as in Anglo-America, the woman is often stereotypically seen as the lesser half of the dominant/dependent, aggressive/passive relationship.[6] These jokes and joking relationships, it has been argued, may help males deal with ambiguities, uncertainties and self-definition. The female, however, is pictured without control of her personal or public world, which is in male hands.

The themes of dirty jokes, as Wilson has pointed out, raise male esteem by comparing themselves "favourably to the butt of the joke."[7] They are expressive of themes of aggression, sexuality, and derision. Dirty jokes and verbal dueling reassure men that they maintain control by laughter. Thoughtful women are seen as humorless because they do not enjoy humor in which the woman is victim. An excellent example of this is the following poem by Veronica Cunningham.

> a woman
> was raped
> by her father
> yesterday
> and she was only
> thirteen
> and
> i never laugh
> at rape jokes
> another woman
> was raped
> on her first date
> and
> i kant laugh
> at rape
> i just kant laugh
> at rape
> another
> was raped
> by a man
> of a different color
>
> political
> perhaps
> fucked
> for sure
> another woman
> by her husband
> but that's
> with the law
> of property

and another
and another
and they have been
violated by more
than a penis

they've suffered
by the law
with policemen
in the courts
in society
inside themselves
with guilt
or shame
because
people believe
the victim
   should be blamed
and i'll be raped
with every
woman
i kant laugh
i kant forget[8]

The perceived lack of control by women is another factor in female nonjoking patterns. Paul McGhee notes that in perceiving humor, "the greatest single source of individual differences may be whether the child is male or female."[9] McGhee attributes the fact that women initiate humor less to the following factors: (1) that clowning and joke telling are seen as socially assertive and women are socialized not to "aggressively dominate mixed-sex social interaction";[10] (2) status has been shown to be relevant to humor initiation, with high-status persons using "other-disparaging humor and low-status persons using self-disparaging humor."[11] He concludes that humorists tend to have more social power than others. Interestingly enough, women tend to laugh at jokes most when the victim is female, perhaps in recognition of and comic relief from their own perceptions of self in society. In addition to the factors suggested by McGhee, I would note that historically women have not initiated jokes and verbal dueling because they have tended to communicate their insecurities and ambivalences in other ways.[12] As one anthropologist commented when she was asked if she told jokes, "I make jokes, but I don't tell them."[13]

Perhaps since women are not socialized to control or because they have not been competitive and aggressive in the same manner as men, their humor has come about not in the public sector (such as in the workplace or the classroom) or on stage (there are very few female comics, and their success has come largely through self-disparaging humor),[14] but rather in the private domain — in the home or in intimate settings where in all likelihood it would not be collected.

> Men's activities usually take place in public arenas, women's in more private ones. As Edwin Ardener notes, "surface structure may express the male view of the world, obscuring the existence at deeper levels of an autonomous female view." Thus, Hannerz found men talking on street corners and Bauman found them talking in a general store, whereas Fernea found women talking behind walls and closed doors. Stoeltje found women's talk performances in homes among friends. Claudia Mitchell-Kernan found female correlates to men's speech (long recognized as performance) both in the home and in mixed group interaction outside the home.
>
> Because the public arenas are more readily accessible than the private ones, it is too often assumed they are the dominant, if not the only, areas where expressive activity occurs. William Ferris succumbs to this trap. After stating that he 'collected primarily from males,' he continues, 'in folklore sessions . . . women never participated unless encouraged by the men present'; he acknowledges that 'if past folklore studies of prose narrative had been done by women rather than men, an extensive 'feminine' tradition . . . might have been recorded."[15]

It is clear, however, that whatever the lack of research on the subject, women's humor does exist. If it is not overwhelmingly seen in the specific form of joke telling or verbal dueling, it comes out in the form of wit and irony. The feminist movement has contributed significantly to equalization in the serious study of women and their culture. Placing value on new ideals and models, this self-equalization has produced a growing body of humor — jokes included, popular and academic — which is other-directed as well as self-directed.

If documentation and study of women's humor in general has been lacking, the study of humor used by minority women is even more ignored. The Chicana is thrice oppressed by virtue of being a woman in a male-dominated culture, a minority in the white/Anglo culture, and because of her own ambivalence of place and state in society. She is struggling to find out who she is and how to define herself within two cultures and two value systems. Coming from a traditional value system, she has to struggle against a fairly rigid stereotype. She should be passive, accepting, enduring, hardworking, and, above all, a good mother, obedient daughter, and faithful wife, always giving of herself to others and never self-directed. For the

Chicana there is also particular emphasis on family orientation and solidarity.

The Chicana *writer,* however, is an anomaly by definition. She is generally educated and professional with aspirations for self-definition on her own terms. To write is to take control, to express your environment, and to break away from acceptance. The pressures on the Chicana writer to adhere to Raza values involve, among other things, not being a feminist. Feminism has been seen in some senses as opposition to traditional values and as "acculturation," selling out to Anglo culture.

Since the Chicano Renaissance, Chicano writers have been expressing a kaleidoscope of perspectives focusing primarily on social conflict and voicing the minority experience in the United States. However, *Chicana* writers have just recently begun to publish, with the volume of material growing significantly only in the last five years. Most write poetry and short stories. Only recently have the first novels begun to emerge. Poetry has always been an acceptable medium for the Latina writer since in it she can express her "emotional, temperamental, affective, and subjective" nature. Many of the writers have not considered themselves feminists because they have remained ideologically devoted to traditional values of caring for family and sticking with their men. This has been generally viewed as necessary to the cause. A criticism of the Mexican-American system or of sexism itself by women is, in effect, a breaking of the ranks of ethnic solidarity and an abandonment of "the culture." Thus, the system creates tremendous pressure and feelings of ambivalence for the writer, feelings which she sometimes expresses directly and sometimes indirectly through humor and irony. For example, movement women felt relegated to the kitchen to fix the beans while the men talked revolution; there are many comments in writing to this effect. Lorna Dee Cervantes writes:

> you speak of the new way,
> a new life . . .
> Pero your voice is lost to me carnal,
> in the wail of tus hijos,
> in the clatter of dishes,
> and the pucker of beans upon the stove.
> Your conversations come to me
> de la sala where you sit,
> spreading your dream to brothers . . .[16]

and Margarita Cota-Cárdenas comments:

> he's very much aware now
>   and makes fervent Revolution
>   so his children
>   and the masses
>   will be free
> but his woman
>   in every language
>   has only begun to ask
>
>   — y yo querido viejo
>   and ME? — [17]

Finding your way is serious business and as one reads Chicana writings one becomes impressed indeed with the lack of humor, the lack of jokes. Some of this can be attributed to the reasons already mentioned for the general lack of humor by women and the rest to the feelings of powerlessness and lack of control that the Chicana feels in a paradoxical society where her language, her culture, and her values are in flux. As Rosa María Névarez comments:

> A lady does not smoke
> a lady does not drink
> a lady does not wink
>   nor does she toke
> And there's no way she can think. [18]

Nevertheless, there is humor emerging in the Chicana's realization of her situation. I believe that as the Chicana continues to write and to explore her place in the world, as she is better able to objectify her position, we will begin to see even more of that tension-releasing device that is humor. The Chicana writer at this stage, however, is hovering between laughing and crying.

The instances of humor found in Chicana writing take different forms. Some are based on language, its use and misuse. Some are based on relationships women have with men, children, and family. Some are based on conflict with society. Still others consist of self-parody or self-deprecating humor but, interestingly, not as much as might be expected. Perhaps this is because the Chicana writer has already broken the stereotype and no longer needs to put herself down. As Bernice Zamora states in "So not to be Mottled":

> You insult me
> When you say I'm
>   Schizophrenic.
> *My* divisions are
> Infinite. [19]

Much of the humor to be found in Chicana writing could be perceived as hostile to males. I believe that the male is only a symbol

of a class of oppressor the woman writer perceives. It is not hostility
we see as much as it is anger. As Sylvia Chacón states, "My poetry is
a struggle to share and convey a glow of warmth and also a bite of
anger to a society that screws copper centered scented daisies in place
within the sterile confines of an assembly line."[20] The problem is how
to deal creatively with that anger. One female humorist states, "the
truth will make you free, but first it will make you miserable. Our
humor turns our anger into a fine art."[21] A young Chicana poet
expresses it in this manner:

> Yo soy mujer. I wish to be one.
> But I no longer like being none.[20]

Let us turn now to a closer examination of the fine line between
laughing and crying in Chicana writing. Childhood is one basis for
amusement in Chicano literature. For many Chicano writers an
examination of childhood is a way of determining roots, reevaluating
meaning, and contrasting values. It is also a period the writer
perceives as being free. Margarita Cota-Cárdenas uses childhood
perceptions to comment on the restrictions the adult faces.[23] She is
also one of the few Chicana poets to consistently use humor and irony
as a more universal recognition of the human condition. On reading
her poem "Nostalgia" we smile because we recognize the perceptions
and fantasies of the child's world.

> I thought then
> that I would like to be a nun with
> long white veil floating in the wind
> mounted on horseback like the actress María Félix
> riding   riding off into
> a lovely cinema type sunset
> in the Convent of the Good Shepherd
> we ate dark cornflakes
> wheaties with coffee and not milk and thus
> poor but pure we would get to be
> instant nuns
> the way I thought one could do everything
> like in the movies of the 1940's
> at the Motor-Vu.[24]

The world of the child is a world of questioning authority and of
rebellion. For a time, at least, the rebellion is accepted until the
norms of society are imposed. Cota-Cárdenas, in this next poem,
paints a portrait of her rebellious sister that is amusing, particularly
in light of the decorous young woman the sister has become.

> that little sister of mine
> was pretty, small tender

but also very brave
she wore cowboy boots
a cowboy hat t-shirt and levis
she was always followed
by little Wienie dogs
the Chapo   the Chapa   and the Chapitos
once she tried to take a molar from one
with a large pair of mechanics' pliers
and during Holy Mass
when communion was offered
to be precise
she said to Father Jean Vincent
—Cabrón. I am going to tell my papa
that you didn't want to give me a
white cookie.

Now
well   she's a mother   wife
and she behaves.[25]

Humor is also used to creatively solve overwhelming problems in the relationship of the individual to a rigid society that seeks to make women submissive and passive. In "The Paris Gown," a short story by Estela Portillo Trambley, we have a brilliant example of this inventiveness. The story centers around a grandmother, Clotilde, living in Paris, and her granddaughter, Theresa, who is visiting her. Clotilde tells Theresa the story of how she was able to live in Paris. Clotilde lived the traditional life of a female in Mexico in the early twentieth century. She had always been, however, very competitive with her brother.

My brother and I used to ride a lot. We had a pair of matched stallions, beautiful horses. Riding along the path of the high hills was an excitement that grew in the body and escaped in the wind. It was a taste of wild freedom. I was the better rider, or maybe it was my greater desire for the wildness that made me the better rider. . . . My father would say . . . A man must never allow a woman to outdo him. How typical of him! The way of the varón and Felix was his varón . . . . I was just a daughter, an after-thought, so I thought. My mother would whisper to me . . . Let your brother win when you race. It would to please your father . . . I did not wish to please my father with the accomplishments of my brother. To outdo him became my constant form of revenge. My father resented the fact and overlooked my ability to outdo, as if it did not exist . . . This was adding salt to my wounds . . .[26]

Felix is allowed to go to Paris to study art, to "sow his wild oats." When Clotilde asks her father what *she* is going to do about her wild oats, he becomes violent and threatens to put her into a nunnery. Soon, however, he finds a better solution:

> He decided to marry me off to a neighboring widower old enough to be my father. Mind you, it was more than just desperation on his part; it was also a good business venture. Don Ignacio was the wealthiest man around. It was the usual contract marriage between parents of means. Daughters did not have a say in the matter. It was an excellent way of joining two fortunes by blood.[27]

Coltilde pleads with her father, saying, "You simply do not unpetal a flower for your advantage. You give it a chance of life!" But her father insists that she marry. Clotilde then demands just one special thing: the most beautiful gown from Paris for the engagement ball.

> When the gown arrived, everybody was excited. It was a maze of tulle and lace and pearl insets. The ultimate of fashion. It was the most beautiful gown anyone had ever seen in that town.[28]

The day of the ball arrives and at 9 PM Clotilde is to descend the stairs, showing off the Paris gown (and Don Ignacio's new possession) to the fullest. She appears at the top of the staircase:

> Immediately, I heard the cries and horrified exclamations among the guests. I thought at the moment of closing my eyes, but I was certain to fall. Also, I did not wish to appear afraid or ashamed, so I tried to look down into their faces. All wore the same frozen, shocked look of disbelief. I saw my mother fall into a faint, and the choleric face of Don Ignacio was punctuated by a fallen jaw of disbelief and anger. He threw his champagne glass and it smashed on the floor, then he turned and left with ceremony. No one noticed his departure, for all eyes were upon me. . . . All this I saw as I came down the stairs . . . stark naked. . . .
>
> It was simple after that. My father could not abandon an insane daughter, but he knew that my presence meant constant reminder. He let me come to Paris with sufficient funds . . . and here I made my home.[29]

The contrast between the beautiful Paris gown (symbolizing woman's role) and the independence of appearing stark naked (casting off rules and regulations) is not only humorous, but also a tribute to the creativity and ingenuity of the solution to the problem. The role model of how to live creatively is then communicated to the grand-daughter, who is the recipient of the "object lesson."

In the same vein, but with more ramifications for the self, is a short poem by Cota-Cárdenas, "Mischievous Soliloquy."

> it's very hard   being a flower
>   sometimes
>   when we're all alone
>   and on the way
>   we concentrate real hard   like this
>   and wrinkle up our brow
>   so that we'll wither beforehand
>   and when we get to the market   hee hee
>   they can't sell us[30]

Bergson finds humor in the comparison of humans to machines. Perhaps we should also include other objects. Women are always being compared to flowers and in some ways are seen as beautiful objects; in the case of Clotilde, they are used as marketable merchandise. The refusal to allow oneself to be sold, or to play the "game," is important to self-concept and self-growth. Here the humor of the poem transmits an in-group message about consciousness and identity.

Male-female relationships also come under comic/tragic scrutiny. The Chicana, as she strives to understand herself, faces some ambiguity in rapidly changing roles with men. The conflict and resulting tension are dealt with by changing the image of the female as she has been stereotyped in society and by a vague feeling of superiority as woman looks down on man for his rigid attitudes. In "Gullible" Cota-Cárdenas reverses the Penelope image, inserting ambiguity as she pokes fun at the stereotype.

> how patiently
>   how lonely
>   you weave your tapestries
>   Penelope
> he's over there Circing himself
>   taking his sweet time
>   you're working so prettily
>   a symbol now of patience
>   slowly   slowly   slowly
>   for so many years   a lovely example
>   weaving   unweaving
>   frustrated years
>   or
> he satisfied you through egotistical telepathy
>   or
>   you had a lover.[31]

Humor is found in the debunking of the myth, the recognition of the humanness of the situation, and in the "put down" of the double standard.

Cota-Cárdenas also comments on romantic beliefs about love:

> The bride is my mother, and she is radiant
> at the lilac and white reception.
> I helped make the potato and macaroni salads,
> refilled the punch bowls, and met
> my all-new, all-blond step brothers and sisters.
> In the family portrait, the assortment of
> fairs and browns, all ages, tried on smiles
> (In wonder who else had cold cuts stuck between
> their teeth?) I'm still wondering if it's
> possibly significant that mother should still
> be the one that believes in fairy tale weddings
> and happily ever after. At her age, she hopes
> sex will still be fun — I figure it can't hurt.[32]

Another poem in this satirical vein, by Lorna Dee Cervantes, derives its humor from touching on taboo subjects as well as from the exaggeration in tone of making the woman into a piece of food (Mexican of course) to be consumed.

> You cramp my style, baby
> when you roll on top of me
> shouting, "Viva la Raza"
> at the top of your prick.
>
> You want me como un taco,
> dripping grease,
> or squeezing masa through my legs,
> making tamales for you
> out of my daughters.
>
> You "mija"
> "mija" "mija" me
> until I can scream
>
> and then you tell me,
> "Esa I LOVE
> this revolution!
> Come on Malinche,
> gimme some more!"[33]

The image of Malinche as betrayer of her people to the Spaniards and Hernán Cortés is one that the Chicana struggles against, since if she is too assimilated into American culture she is considered a sellout (and, as stated before, feminism is one way of selling out).

Marina Rivera takes on the male/female relationship by self-parody in "The Lion Tamer's Wife." The woman's anger gradually turns her into a voracious animal that the husband must deal with at the end of the day.

At breakfast
tries to hide her growing claws,
points as yet minute, tentative.

At lunch
as claws hang up in the tea cups
only her eyes roar.

By dinner
he finds her perched high,
a voice louder than cannon,
angling one arm down wanting
a small piece of scalp
for her barrel mouth,
savoring her equal rights
and his amendment.[34]

The last characteristic of Chicana humor I would like to discuss is linguistic humor. Because many Chicanos write in both English and Spanish, occasions arise to make humorous plays on words, meanings, and their proper use and misuse. Sociolinguistic commentary is contained in a long poem by la Chrisx, "La loca de la Raza Cósmica," where the poet is trying to define all the things a woman represents to both cultures. The code switching between English and Spanish creates humorous juxtapositions. It also emphasizes the Chicana's ambivalent feelings toward two value systems that are often in conflict:

soy mujer
soy señorita
soy ruca loca
soy mujerona
soy santa
soy madre
soy ms.
        . . .
soy shacking up
soy staying at home until I'm married
        or dead
soy dumping my old man, even though I'm
        pregnant with his child
soy getting married in Reno with the
        kids at home
soy getting married with 15 bridesmaids
        and champagne and cake
soy mother of 12, married at 14
soy staying together for the kids' sakes
soy la que se chinga pa' mantener a su
        familia

> soy marianismo, living to love and support
>   my husband and to nurture and teach
>   my children
> soy la battered wife
>   . . .
> soy 'tank you' en vez de thank you
> soy 'chooz' en vez de shoes
> soy refinada-educated in assimilated/
>   anglicized/private institutions
>   . . .
> soy la que va a visitar al pinto
> soy la que piensa que un pinto, es a bean.[35]

The clash/convergence of cultures and value judgements leads to a complex linguistic/cultural tension that becomes particularly acute in the last phrase. The poet pokes fun at the assimilated Mexican American who often does not speak Spanish, looks down on the culture, and would not know that in slang a pinto is a prisoner in jail and not something to eat. The expressed attitude about ethnicity is that even if you are assimilated, you must be proud of your culture, your traditions, and your language.

Cota-Cárdenas plays linguistically with those illusions and fantasies women have about the perfect lover who will fulfill their lives:

> "Justo Será"
> días   semanas   meses
>   sin saber de
>   poetizados espasmos
> todo por creer
>   en los caballeros-andantes
>
>   aquel pinchi bato
> y su mitificado horse
>   coming down the camino-brick-road
>   with a mecate-rope
>   around his pescuezo-neck
> que nunca
>   nunca
>   llega
>
> "It must be just"
> days   weeks   months
>   without knowing
>   poetic spasms
> all for believing
>   in knights in shining armor
>   that damn guy

and his mythified horse
   coming down the camino-brick-road
   with a mecate-rope
   around his pescuezo-neck
that never
    never
      gets here[36]

The caricature of the woman awaiting her knight is heightened by the code switching/culture switching of the poem, evoking not only the tales of chivalry so beloved in Spanish culture but also the Wizard of Oz (camino-brick-road/yellow brick road) and the cowboy mystique. The absurd juxtaposition pokes fun at the clash of culture and illusions. We laugh because we recognize our foibles, we laugh at the reflection of our image. Laughing at our belief systems, our myths, our struggles, and our responses makes the situation more human.

Mary Douglas has stated that "the joke connects and disorganizes. It attacks sense and hierarchy."[37] The joker lightens for everyone the oppressiveness of social reality, demonstrates its arbitrariness by making light formality in general, and expresses the creative possibilities of the situation. Yet, Chicana writing constantly walks the thin line between laughing and crying. When tension that has built up is released in laughter, it is almost immediately followed by a sobering image. It is as if the writers desire to string out the heightened awareness to emphasize that nothing has been resolved.

It is interesting to note that except for a few put-downs of Anglo culture, Chicana humor is not so much aimed at feelings of ethnicity or even at the dominant culture but rather, on a more personal level, at the realities of everyday living and at the poor self-image the Chicana has of herself. It strives to break the cultural stereotype. It also tries to deal with the anger the Chicana feels in her relationships with men and the ambiguity she tries to resolve as she is caught between two cultures: does she sell out by continuing to define and seek herself? or does she sell herself out by adhering to traditional norms?

Humor in Chicana writing does, I believe, the following things:

(1)   It conveys a different point of view, that is, the female perspective on life "as it is."

(2)   It struggles against the stereotype, asserting the infinite complexities of women. The new Penelope stands on equal footing.

(3)   It releases some of the tension the writer feels about ambivalent or conflict situations. The most conflictive is

whether to break away from traditional behavior patterns in order to be free to define oneself. The humor that we might define as feminist helps her to define her own terms. As Mary Kay Blakely says, "With our humor we learn how to live in a society, despite its sexism, without compromising too many of our principles or sacrificing too much of our happiness. We use our humor as a cure for burn out."[38]

(4) It reinforces the writer's identification with the group as a woman and as a Chicana. It solidifies in-group feeling and increases morale.

(5) It functions as a creative release from too much anger.

(6) It gives insights into the Chicana sociocultural experience and may be appreciated because "It provides a temporary respite from the absurdity of one's predicament."[39]

(7) It functions as a model for change. Humor not only serves to criticize the social system but also to criticize behavior on the part of the Chicana herself. It evokes amusement and contempt against the perpetrator of an inflexible system and also against the woman (oneself) for allowing it. The ridicule is shared by all of us who laugh at our common predicament. This recognition is a call for action and for change.

As the Chicana continues to write and to strive for social as well as personal equality, I believe she will increasingly use humor in her writing. To be creative about anger and frustration takes time and a bit of distance from the "front line." Kaufman succinctly states: "By joking, we rehumanize, recivilize ourselves. By joking, we remake ourselves so that after each disappointment we become once again capable of living and loving."[40]

UNIVERSITY OF NEW MEXICO

Notes

[1]As cited in Charles I. Glickesberg, *The Ironic Vision in Modern Literature* (The Hague: Martinus Nijhoff, 1969), p. 3.

[2]Gloria Kaufman and Mary Kay Blakely, *Pulling Our Own Strings* (Bloomington: Indiana University Press, 1980), pp. 15-16.

[3]Carol Mitchell, "Hostility and Aggression Towards Males in Female Joke Telling." *Frontiers,* 3:3 (1978), 19-23; Carol Mitchell, "The Female Perspective in the

Appreciation and Interpretation of Jokes." *Western Folklore,* 36: 4 (1977), 303-330; Paul McGhee, "Sex Differences in Children's Humor." *Journal of Communication,* 26 (1976), 176-189.

⁴An important exception is the excellent article by Rafaela Castro, "Mexican Women's Sexual Jokes." *Aztlán,* 13:1-2 (1982), 275-293.

⁵Alan Dundes, J.W. Leach, and B. Ozkok, "The Strategy of Turkish Boys' Dueling Rhymes." *Journal of American Folklore,* 76 (1970), 111-118; Américo Paredes, "The Anglo-American in Mexican Folklore," In Antonia Castañeda Shular, ed., *Literatura Chicana: Texto y Contexto* (Englewood Cliffs, NJ: Prentice-Hall, 1972), pp. 141-150.

⁶Américo Paredes and Joseph Spielberg, "Humor in a Mexican-American Palomilla." Unpublished paper delivered to the American Anthropological Association, 1973.

⁷Christopher P. Wilson, *Jokes: Form, Content, Use and Fiction* (London: Academic Press, 1979), p. 153.

⁸Veronica Cunningham, "A Woman was raped." *Capirotada* (1977), 43.

⁹McGhee, p. 201.

¹⁰*Ibid.,* p. 202. See also Rose Coser, "Laughter Among Colleagues." *Psychiatry,* 23 (1970), 81-89.

¹¹Joan B. Levine, "The Feminine Routine." *Journal of Communication,* 26 (1976), 173-175.

¹²For a fascinating commentary on how women communicate, see Susan Kalčik, ". . . like Ann's gynecologist or the time I was almost raped." In Claire R. Farrer, ed., *Women and Folklore* (Austin: University of Texas Press, 1975), pp. 3-11.

¹³Comment to the author, July 27, 1981.

¹⁴Levine, pp. 173-175.

¹⁵Farrer, p. xi.

¹⁶Lorna Dee Cervantes, in Dexter Fisher, ed., *The Third Woman. Minority Women Writers of the United States* (Boston: Houghton Mifflin, 1980), pp. 381-382.

¹⁷Margarita Cota-Cárdenas, in *La Palabra,* 2:2 (1980), 40.

¹⁸Rosa María Névarez, in *Capirotada* (1977), 1.

¹⁹Bernice Zamora, *Restless Serpents* (Menlo Park, CA: Diseños Literarios, 1976), p. 42.

²⁰Sylvia Chacón, in *Capirotada* (1977), 21.

²¹Mary Kay Blakely, in Kaufman, p. 12.

²²Raquel Rodríguez, "Yo soy mujer." *Comadre,* II (1978), 18.

²³See Tey Diana Rebolledo, "The Bittersweet Nostalgia of Childhood in the Poetry of Margarita Cota-Cárdenas." *Frontiers,* 5:2 (1980), 31-35.

²⁴*Ibid.,* p. 32.

²⁵*Ibid.,* p. 34.

²⁶Estela Portillo [Trambley], *Rain of Scorpions* (Berkeley: Tonatiuh International, 1975), p. 5.

²⁷*Ibid.,* p. 6.

²⁸*Ibid.,* p. 7.

²⁹*Ibid.,* p. 8.

³⁰Margarita Cota-Cárdenas, *Noches despertando inConciencias* (Tucson: Scorpion Press, 1975), p. 29.

³¹Margarita Cota-Cárdenas, in Fisher, p. 399.

³²Margarita Cota-Cárdenas, unpublished poem, 1979.

[33]Lorna Dee Cervantes, "You Cramp My Style, Baby." *Fuego de Aztlán*, 1:4 (1977), 40.

[34]Marina Rivera, "The Lion Tamer's Wife." *Caracol*, 5:9 (1979), 5.

[35]La Chrisx, in *Comadre*, 2 (Spring 1978), 2.

[36]Cota-Cárdenas, in Rebolledo, p. 34.

[37]Mary Douglas, "The Social Control of Cognition: Some Factors in Joke Perception." *Man*, 3 (1968), 371.

[38]Blakely, in Kaufman, p. 12.

[39]Jeffrey H. Goldstein, "Theoretical Notes on Humor." *Journal of Communication*, 26 (1976), 102.

[40]Kaufman, p. 16.

THE BIRTHING OF THE POETIC "I"
IN ALMA VILLANUEVA'S *MOTHER, MAY I?*:
THE SEARCH FOR A FEMININE IDENTITY

Marta E. Sánchez

Of the major Chicana poets, Alma Villanueva is the most consciously preoccupied with a search for a "universal" feminine community. The influence of the woman's movement in the United States seems to have come to her without significant interference from the Chicano social movement of the same period. Like the other poets, Villanueva is the product of a socialization process; yet, her overriding objective as a poet is to transform her concrete experiences into a vision of a personalized myth, an objective she achieves in *Mother, May I?*[1]

Before *Mother, May I?* appeared in 1978, Alma Villanueva had published in 1977 two poetic personal biographies, *Bloodroot*[2] and the Irvine *Poems*.[3] That same year, *Poems* was named the first place winner in poetry of the Chicano Literary Prize competition at the University of California, Irvine. These collections reveal that Villanueva is a poet who senses a development of herself in time. She is, in fact, not only the most sequential in presentation among such major poets as Lorna Dee Cervantes and Bernice Zamora, but also the only one to write a poetic autobiography. This achievement also makes her unique among Chicano poets. Well-known male poets like Gary Soto, José Montoya, Tino Villanueva, and Raúl Salinas have written personal poems that capture fragments of their lives, but not one of these poets has written a sustained narrative sequence in lyric form. Alma Villanueva does exactly this. In *Mother, May I?*, her most interesting and dynamic work, she retraces the important phases of her life from childhood to her early thirties.

In comparison with the other two Chicana poets mentioned above, I suspect that Alma Villanueva has the most need to write an autobiographical poem. Since the autobiography necessitates a retrospective look at a person's life and an explanation of how authors arrive where they do, such an endeavor offers Villanueva the opportunity to confront some compelling questions about her personal formation that stand in the way of a desired poetic vision. The theme of a mother's abandonment is certainly the overriding concern of *Mother, May I?* A second theme is the unknown father—Villanueva never knew or saw her father. She did learn later in life, though, that her father was of German descent. And though it is the search for a mother, and not a father, that plays the central part in the poet's quest for self-definition in *Mother, May I?*, the issue of mixed and ambiguous origins is a biographical detail that conditions the result of the poetic peregrination.

In light of such fundamental absences as those of a mother and a father, it is understandable why Villanueva's protagonist in *Mother, May I?* must achieve the birthing of a personal self, or her "I." The absence of a mother may also help to explain why femininity is linked with the eternal and timeless. Villanueva's quest for a continuous and fluid participation in a mythical, feminine community may come from a deeper wish to transcend the interruptions she perceived to mar the relations with her real mother. A maternal Mexican grandmother raised her until she was eleven years old, a biographical fact that accounts for her emotional identification with Mexican culture. This emotional identification is connected to childhood. A Chicana identity forms a minor part of her adult poetic persona. Villanueva's poetic identity lies more within a community bonded by gender than one bonded by race and ethnicity.

When compared with the poetry of Lorna Dee Cervantes and Bernice Zamora, Villanueva's contains the least presence of a Chicana consciousness. Villanueva's response to the double dilemma of being both a woman and a Chicana is to respond primarily as a woman to dominant "masculine" society.[4] Her primary intent is to reveal and express an intimate record of her individual existence as a woman to other women rather than to communicate the experiences of a communal group to a larger audience, as is Lorna Dee Cervantes' goal. The tension in Villanueva's poetic world is manifested at the level of a personal quest to achieve self-definition as a woman. In *Mother, May I?*, Villanueva's journey in search of her womanhood is also a journey in search of her poetic identity.

While no significant conflict dramatizes the relationship between Villanueva's identities as woman and Chicana (as it does in Bernice Zamora), they are not totally integrated with one another either (as they are in Lorna Dee Cervantes). These two identities are characterized by a relationship of juxtaposition rather than fusion in her poetic voice. The disjuncture in the poetic voice is embodied by various shifts in focus adopted by the poetic persona: from past to present moments, from an urban to a rural setting, from linear to circular time, from a social-documentary style to a metaphoric-mythic style. In *Mother, May I?* a sequential progression of events is disrupted in favor of a more fluid and subjective reality.

As fragmented attempts to confront the realities and desires of her life, *Bloodroot* and *Poems* prepare Villanueva to write *Mother, May I?* In the former two collections, she attempts to make a statement of her development as a woman and a poet by juxtaposing a personal, documentary voice with a mythic, "universal" voice. The first voice speaks about her social reality and the second articulates where she desires to be. In *Mother, May I?* she establishes a linear sequence to the narration of her life using the personal, documentary voice to express her past life, and the mythic, "universal" voice to express her present life. In *Mother, May I?* she arrives at her objective and speaks from where she is.

Although Villanueva confesses a familiarity with Pablo Neruda but not with Walt Whitman prior to the publication of *Bloodroot,* Whitmanesque tones, imagery, and the theme of cosmic unity predominate in this collection.[5] Whitman, we know, was a major influence on Neruda during the period of 1925-36 when he was writing *Residencia en la tierra.*[6] Villanueva read in translation and admired *Residencia en la tierra* and *Veinte poemas de amor* (1924). A Whitmanesque voice is especially manifest in *Bloodroot* when Villanueva speaks about her body, and by extension, all women's bodies. While both Whitman and Neruda are noted for speaking about their bodies in their poetry, they did so in different ways: Whitman used a celebratory tone, giving his body cosmic proportions; Neruda employed a humorous, metaphysical tone, stressing its materiality.[7] Neruda did, however, adopt a cosmic, pantheistic description of the female body in *Veinte poemas* and in the erotic poems of *Residencia,* where he presents woman's body as a microcosm of the world, a veritable force of the universe.[8] Villanueva's celebration of her body, then, coincides more with Neruda's vision of the feminine body than it does with that of his own. His description of his body reveals a consciousness of the materiality of the human organism. Her celebratory tone does, however, coincide with Whitman's tone and attitude.

In my discussion of *Bloodroot*, I stress Whitman over Neruda as one of Villanueva's main influences because the totality of Villanueva's poetry reveals stronger connections with an Anglo-American literary tradition than with a Latin American and Chicano literary heritage. The mythic tones of Neruda's description of the female body probably proved congenial with Villanueva's poetic sensibilities. In an indirect way, Villanueva taps Whitman and her North American roots via her reading of Neruda.

Poems demonstrates influences from contemporary American woman poets, especially Sylvia Plath and Anne Sexton. Villanueva's poems are more loosely organized than those of either Plath or Sexton.[9] Throughout *Mother, May I?* she employs short lines, at times seemingly inattentive to where she breaks them. Other times, a mere broken line suffices to signal abrupt shifts in focus and tone. Villanueva uses neither Plath's clinical precision of image nor the tight stanzaic and metrical patterns of "Lady Lazarus" and "Daddy." More oral, more presentational in tone than Plath or Sexton, she desires to remove the mediations between the speaker and the addressee. Her predominantly colloquial tone is characterized by different variants or gradations. One variant is a childish and infantile language, a kind of little-girl baby talk that becomes a way of reliving the joys and pains of childhood. A second variant of her colloquial tone is the bawdy, which is most pronounced in some of the *Bloodroot* poems and those of the Irvine collection. Her bawdy language gives testimony that, like some of her Anglo women contemporaries, Villanueva is interested in invading traditional male linguistic preserves.[10]

Since the form of the autobiography calls for a more self-conscious and self-reflective appraisal of the poetic "I," Villanueva is better able in *Mother, May I?* than in *Bloodroot* or *Poems* to scrutinize and analyze her "I" as a mediated presence. In this poetic narrative she reveals that she has become more conscious of the formation and constraints of her narrative and poetic voice. For this reason, *Mother, May I?* is less derivative than the earlier poems. Villanueva's desire to write an autobiographical poem might then be inspired indirectly by Whitman. At the formal level, Villanueva's poetic autobiography combines Whitman with Plath and Sexton. If Whitman provides the genre, then Plath and Sexton provide the mode. Villanueva employs the confessional mode in modified form to disclose the private and intimate details of her life.

The poetic enterprise of *Mother, May I?* will be to create from concrete experience a personal myth of a "universal" womanhood. As an autobiographical poem, the narrating consciousness of *Mother, May I?* must incorporate both identities of woman and Chicana into the poetic voice. I treat the poem here as a self-sufficient entity, unmoored from the context that conditioned it.[11] The poem is a fictional composition of events and actions that explain the coming into being of the protagonist as poet. By doing a close reading of the poem as a verbal artifact, or a string of words that reverberate and echo one another, I argue that *Mother, May I?* successfully integrates the identities of woman and Chicana into the poet's "I."

"Bloodroot" and the Irvine "Poems"

Bloodroot is a kind of poetic journal, a hasty jotting down of notes, impressions, and ideas. Many of its themes are cosmic. Full of carnal and elemental images (blood, womb, stones, plants, minerals, water), these poems express Villanueva's nostalgic desire for reintegration with an original, maternal womb from which, presumably, both women and men emerged. The feminine body is portrayed as a Jungian archetype. Villanueva's feminine speakers "celebrate" and "rejoice" in women's bodies and wombs, urging everyone, but especially men, to recognize their connection with their material bond. A few lines from her poem "(woman)"[12] are representative:

> (wo)man
>   Yes Woman!
> I celebrate our bodies,
> our wombs,
> intact and perfect even as
> we're born
> out of our mother's
>   womb
> I celebrate
> because most   . . . If man is out
> men have forgotten   of touch with
> how to   the earth,
> he is afraid   how can he
> of us, he   touch woman)[13]
> denies us.
>   —but in the process
>   denies his own existence;
>   when will he re/learn
>   this ancient fact—

Villanueva's mythic "I" in this poem shifts into a "we" that desires to speak about and to all women. Her "I" proudly asserts her body's functions ("the slick / red walls of our / wombs, / the milk of our breasts / the ecstasy of our clitoris") while her "we" defines categorically the essence of women:

> we are the trees of the earth
> our roots stretching deep and srong,
> the stone of the firmament,
> sister to the stars
> that gave birth to the soil.

The title poem "bloodroot"[14] expresses a woman's fantasy to experience a mystic pregnancy, one independent of any interaction with male powers. Using Whitmanesque tones and images, the female persona calls upon trees, wind, and birds to perform the male reproductive act. Ecstatic and exuberant, she receives, as in a trance, the "sperm" of trees and the nectar of hummingbirds. Bitterness and sweetness are conjoined in her.

> bloodroot
> I grow heavy with the sperm
> of trees,
> with the nectar
> of hummingbirds (listen to their
> motor, purring)
> with the journeying
> wind, it
> fills me
> and tiny kisses cover
> my eyes, my neck,
> my leafy hair: roots
>
> threaten to form;
> my toes ache;
> my eyes shut
> and chrysalis begins. I
> see the sun in a
> bloody pattern: colors dance.
> different eyes will open
> and my roots are wise; they
> love me, but not
> too well.
>
> I grow heavy with the sperm
> of trees.

The speaker celebrates the awakening of a mythic female consciousness and foreshadows the creation of a primal world where the blood of woman will be the root of all life. The images in "bloodroot" convey a parallel between the speaker's body and the earth: "My leafy hair"; "my eyes shut / and chrysalis begins." The sun is associated with blood, a source of life in women's bodies: "I / see the sun in a / bloody pattern." Since "chrysalis" begins, the woman is in a process of becoming, but not yet at the point of full maturation. "Bloodroot" externalizes a woman's inner wish to birth alone. In the poem's title, Villanueva joins two different words together to call attention to the indissociable relationship of their meanings in her poetic world. She uses this same technique in the poem "ZINZ,"[15] where she locates the feminine creatrix in a non-Western "motherafrica." The neologism emphasizes the idea of union among all men and women.

> we were
> collectively, together
>   born
>   out of
>   motherafricas
>   womb.

In the early poems of *Bloodroot,* Villanueva desires to recover the resonance of nature and to restore to her readers an awareness of their interdependence with the feminine universe. She also desires to birth independently of a masculine power. Villanueva repeats these themes again and again in modified ways throughout *Bloodroot.* Although they did so in different ways, her masculine inspirators, Neruda and Whitman, energetically chronicled an awakening consciousness for their countries. Villanueva attempts to chronicle an awakening consciousness of a mythical womanhood. As Whitman urged humanity to reestablish its connection to the natural universe, so, in a similar way, Villanueva urges her audience to reestablish its lost connection to a feminine, magisterial cosmos.

Villanueva's poetic voice changes even as she writes *Bloodroot* and the Irvine *Poems.* A more personal and autobiographical voice emerges midway through *Bloodroot.* In "I sing to myself,"[16] Villanueva takes up Whitman's dictum that poetry should occasion a reader's composing a song of oneself.[17] This poem gives evidence that Villanueva has begun to confront the paradox of her objective: to sing her spontaneous, natural song of beauty and wonder, she must first confront her own feelings of bitterness and distrust. The opening metaphor of an "over-ripe fruit" represents those feelings that keep her from speaking and releasing her song.

> I sing to myself
> there is something
> I carry deep

within me
like an over-ripe
fruit, one whose use is past and
won't rot and merge
and gags me
now and then;
      it is the fruit
of bitterness and distrust.
   oh yes, they planted the seed, but
I tend the soil . . .

The middle stanzas identify in direct, declarative language the refer-
ent of *they* above: a father who never loved her ("I could weep and
rage / against the man who never / . . . desired me in a secret
fathers / way");[18] a mother who spent all her energies needing and desiring men ("never finding a breast to rest / and warm myself"); and a
self-centered husband (who "loved me at his leisure and / neglected
my deepest needs"). The final lines return to metaphorically fore-
shadow her transformation as the new Eve who will birth herself by
swallowing and transforming the putrid fruit.

I will swallow you whole and
accept and transform you
till you melt
in my mouth.   (you/man only
        bit the apple:
           you must swallow
      death —
            I/woman give birth:
              and this time to
    myself)

This poem juxtaposes the two voices that will make up
Villanueva's poetic identity in *Mother, May I?* Here, the mythical
voice allows her to express a vision of herself transfigured as the new
Eve and the private voice to express her unhappy personal life. These
two voices never merge or fuse in "I sing to myself," a division which
indicates the distance between where she is and her goal of
transcendence. As yet, there is only talk of transformation. The
parallel between Adam biting the apple and the new Eve birthing herself is also important. The act of incorporating objects by eating them
will become a sustained image pattern in *Mother, May I?*

The feminine persona of "in your body,"[19] a later poem in
Bloodroot, shows attempts at individuation. The frame of this poem is
mythic, but in contrast to the women speakers of "bloodroot,"
"(wo)man," and "ZINZ" who assume the existence of a feminine

primal cosmos, the speaker of this poem realizes that if she is to gain such a paradise, she must first struggle toward it and earn it. The poem draws an analogy between a woman's sexual orgasm and the process of evolution. Coitus is not simply an act between one man and one woman but the recapitulation of the creation of the entire universe, or a clashing between earth and ocean.

> in your body
>   I found
> the oceans of the earth
> saltless seas of distant planets
> lava flow of the first eruption
> that created
> the first mound of earth
> from the waters
>   the lonely stormy waters
> before earth was born —
> in you/me I felt creations hot hard urgency
> to be
>   and I slept in swirling waters
> floated in stagnant seas
> cradled and crushed by the tides
> your salty semen rushing
> over my shores, leaving me pregnant and
> exhausted in its wake,
>   full of you, the saltysea.
>
> storms & seasons & shifting sun & tide find
>   us separate:
>
> and my own body
> feels the tide
> a relentless gentle/fierce tide
> and I wait at my shore for
> a perfect, whole seashell
> to cast up on the tide
>   aeons of time in the
>   making and forming
>   of this perfect
>
>   shell
>
>   shaped like a
> star.

The consciousness of the poem moves from a description of the woman's sexual orgasm with the cosmic lover's body (stanza 1) into a statement of separation (stanza 2) and finally into a description of the woman waiting alone to toss up the "perfect seashell." The image of the seashell represents either a child or a poem or both. This poem prefigures the pattern of opening and closing that will pervade in

Mother, May I?, suggested here by the tide's ebb and flow and the biological rhythm of the woman's reproductive cycle.

The more personal, private poems in *Bloodroot* are based on autobiographical incidents and describe relationships with key figures in the poet's childhood and youth—her mother, her aunt, and the Mexican grandmother who was so important to her. The fictional world of these poems is neither "timeless" nor "universal" as in the mythic poems. Rather, these poems describe a finite, temporal, and more overtly subjective world. From its place in ordinary, everyday settings, the poetic consciousness, nevertheless, expresses its longing for personal transfiguration. In "I was a skinny tomboy kid,"[20] for example, the persona reflects on her adolescent years when she saw herself as a fated victim because of her female identity. Consequently, she desired instead to be a man, equating her masculinity or tomboy activities (climbing roofs and fences, walking down streets with tightly clenched fists) with freedom, movement, strength, and hardness and her femininity with helplessness, standing still, softness, and letting go: "I vowed / to never / grow up / to be a woman / and be helpless / like my mother." The adult persona, in retrospect, recognizes what she did not see years earlier: "but then I didn't realize / the kind of guts / it often took / for her [mother] to just keep / standing / where she was." Her unhappy childhood led her to create a "legendary / self," "believing in my own myth / transforming my reality." Throughout the poems of *Bloodroot,* the private voice searches for a continuous harmony that can help her overcome the discontinuous quality of her concrete life. She often looks for it in forms of nature and cultural objects: in the bison whose "hooves remember the ancient joy"; in "green bean sprouts . . . intimately connected to the earth"; in the "dazzling beauty of a piñata."

Along the axis established by the personal, private voice, we find in *Bloodroot* a small number of poems that express her social identity as a Chicana. Of the forty-seven poems in *Bloodroot*, five are dedicated to relationships with her Mexican grandmother and aunt. These poems are all situated in particular, concrete circumstances, many of which are recognizably Chicano for an audience familiar with the locations. References to Market and Guerrero Streets, to the Mission District, and to welfare lines and clinics define an urban, Chicano, working-class context in the San Francisco Bay area. In "you cannot leave,"[21] tensions between the Mexican and Anglo worlds are present in the story of her aunt trying to go to an Anglo church, but "their [Anglo] faces were blank and their eyes mute; they did not recognize her." In "to Jesus Villanueva, with love,"[22] a poem about her grandmother, the speaker claims that the main rule of Anglo society is "to lie, to push, to get." So, she lies and pushes to make a doctor examine her ailing grandmother, to convince the welfare office to send her grandmother's check on time, and to persuade the landlady to spray her grandmother's house for cockroaches.

In this same poem she presents a humorous anecdote she heard from her mother about how her grandmother outwitted a border official. The "you" in this passage is the author's grandmother.

> you were leaving Mexico
> with your husband and two
> older children, pregnant
> with my mother.
> the U.S. customs officer
> undid everything you so
> preciously packed, you
> took a sack, blew it up
> and when he asked about
> the contents of the sack,
> well, you popped it with
> your hand and shouted
>   MEXICAN AIR!

I assume that the grandmother told the story to her daughter in Spanish and that the mother then communicated it in English to her daughter, except for the phrase "Mexican air." The daughter-author, then, recounts it to us in English, translating even the phrase "Mexican air," as her footnote states.[23]

In the initial lines of "to Jesus Villanueva," she remembers naming the cultural products of her grandmother's world.

> my first vivid memory of you
> mamacita,
> we made tortillas together
> yours, perfect and round
> mine, irregular and fat
> we laughed
> and named them: oso, pajarito, gatito.

Though the first anecdote is mediated by the mother, both these anecdotes involving her grandmother originally occurred in Spanish. The grandmother is the link to the poet's identification with Mexican-Chicano culture and the Spanish language. Since the narrator recounts in English her experience of naming objects in Spanish with her grandmother, she *tells* of her involvement in this linguistic activity rather than *performs* it.

These poems reveal a speaker who is aware of a separation

between Anglo and Mexican-Chicano cultures. The poet's voice, as it relates to a Chicana identity, is almost always associated in *Bloodroot* — as it will be also in *Mother, May I?* — with her grandmother and her early childhood. The mythical voice envisioning a feminine, cosmic world and the biographical voice desiring personal transfiguration are always associated in *Bloodroot* with Villanueva's quest for a feminine identity. These two identities appear juxtaposed rather than synthesized, expressive of one or the other identity but never fused.

Most of the poems in *Bloodroot* reveal Villanueva's preoccupation with defining her identity as a woman and as a poet. Whitmanesque energy, tones, and incantation help her to express and celebrate the birth and beauties of her womanhood, much as Whitman in an earlier period celebrated the birth and growth of a country. These Whitmanesque mythic strains, however, do not permit her to integrate into her celebration of womanhood an expression of the particularity of her Chicana self.

Poems revises *Bloodroot* because Villanueva's persona reflects a consciousness of where she has been in the past. In *Poems* Villanueva turns to her two feminine models and adapts their literary persona of the poet-narrator as witch, a wild and threatening woman.[24] Villanueva acknowledges her feminine inspirators in "The Last Words,"[25] dedicated to "Anne and Sylvia / and all those that burned before them / in Salem and other places." The theme of woman as witch continues in a somewhat altered form from the mythical strain of *Bloodroot* in that the tradition of the woman as witch evokes mysterious and magical contexts. The identity of the woman as witch/bitch represents the opposite pole of the woman as creatrix, the primal earth mother of the early poems in *Bloodroot*. Villanueva employs this witch persona to taunt and satirize men, those "self-proclaimed gods, priests and oracles." This mocking tone is an indication of her increased awareness since writing the more naive poems modeled on Whitmanesque vocabulary and imagery.

In *Poems* Villanueva defines her feminine "I" by resisting and opposing male society. In "The Last Words" she quotes the final stanza of Plath's "Lady Lazarus," the only stanza of that poem with an explicit reference to men.

> *Out of the ash*
> *I rise with my red hair*
> *and I eat men like air.*

The witch as poet-narrator describes a "hysterical mob" that would like to burn her at the stake for daring to utter notions about the human condition that society wants to repress: "The hysterical mob does not like to be / reminded of their true natures — / they would like to forget women like me." However, the poet-witch must write what she must, just as,

> witches' blood must flow: dry and crackle —
> sink into the mother, turn to ash —
> red fire / blood release the utterance —

Though the crowd may want to set the torch to her, the truth is "they do not know I burn, self/imposed / in a fire of my / own making." Her fire is the "heat" or energy of love, of words, and of blood propelling her to write the poem: "my witches' secret: the poem as / my witness." Her poems, as well as those of Plath and Sexton, "cannot be destroyed. / they burn in the heart / long after the witch is dead." Villanueva never explicitly identifies her enemies as men in this poem, but her use of Plath's line to begin the poem — "and I eat men like air" — suggests that she, like Plath, sees her enemies as men. She sees herself outwitting them by performing the daring ruse of self-immolation that they do not expect.

The tone of bravado against men is more pronounced in "witches' blood," "Of Utterances," and "Of/to Man."[26] In "Of/to Man" she boasts of woman's power to have numerous sexual orgasms at once, since "(spiritual orgasms count too)."

> you're limited to one
> at a time. Is that the
> main bitch?
> well man, my man —
> let's set herstory
> straight. I come IN my cunt
> IN my clit, you might say
> my whole body is IN the
> act.

At the conclusion of "witches' blood," Villanueva's female monster flaunts to the "priests" and the "poets" her preference for a witch identity rather than the one of goddess they have given to her. Taunting them with a series of directives —

> call me witch
> call me hag
> call me sorceress
> call me mad
> call me woman.   do not
> call me goddess
> I do not want the position.

— she openly adores in herself what men have called unclean in women: "I prefer to gaze in wonder / once a month at my / witches' blood." She critically denounces men who "have killed / made war / for blood to flow, as naturally / as a woman's once a month." The poem "witches' blood" originally appeared in *Bloodroot*, but Villanueva now inserts it into the Irvine collection. This action of reverting back to old poems and placing them next to new poems underscores Villanueva's technique of juxtaposition, a technique that becomes more meaningful in *Mother, May I?*

The desire to birth the utterance or poem becomes the compelling theme of the Irvine collection. In "Of Utterances" Villanueva accepts Sexton's advice that a woman must become her own muse. Using ribald humor, she makes a conscious attack on a theory of poetry that cultivates the myth of woman as the inspirational source of white male poets.[27]

> the "White Goddess"
> to white men
> to poets and men of genius
> "a source of inspiration;
> a guiding genius . . ."
> that beautiful goddess
> that legendary angel

She goes on to describe with parodic tones the "legendary Angel" who descends:

> with her milky white limbs,
> full breasts, rosy at the
> tips with the milky
> stanzas and lyrics
> to the touch of man:
> the cunt all acceptance,   opening wide
> to the mind of man   and
> giving birth to their children
> The Poem.   The Painting.   The Sculpture.

After the above satiric litany, she interjects:

> and I with my fetish for dark men
> and dislike (dis-taste) for sucking (this part's o.k. —
> cocks and swallowing the salty sperm (this part's not —
> of prose and rhymes.

She raises the possibility that she too might have to copulate with a "White God" just as her white make predecessors have done with the "White Goddess." Acknowledgement of her fetish for dark men, however, implies some awareness of herself as different from the tradition of white poets. She, a woman-poet with a fetish for dark men, cannot accept this white male model of artistic creation. Her images of "sucking cocks" and "swallowing the salty sperm" of "prose and rhymes" parody the male poet who "copulates" with his white muse to produce his art. They also suggest a self-parody because she, metaphorically speaking, had "sucked upon" and "swallowed" Whitman's cosmic imagery and tones in her earlier poetry. Her mocking tone indicates that she now has enough distance to question a white male literary tradition before naively accepting it.

She further undermines and ridicules the stylized gesture of the white male poet invoking his angelic goddess with an unexpected deviation that substitutes African Black gods as muses of women poets. Her suggestion is that *if* Black gods did exist, she might accept them as sources of creative inspiration. She only makes this gesture, however, to gain ironic effects because she no sooner proposes the option of Black gods as women's muses than she declares it nonexistent: "we women just don't have any / dark and lovely / descending / 'Black Gods.' " Her resolution is to use her own "resources and imagination" and become her own "source of inspiration: my very own genius."

> I grew my own wings, became my
> own muse.
> I decided to fly
> and not descend.

Villanueva identifies with Plath and Sexton in their challenge to the white male ego and his literary discourse. However, she introduces the dimension of the non-white male and his literary tradition by suggesting the possibility of "Black Gods" as muses. She sees herself in the center of an opposition between "white male" and "black male" or between "dominant tradition" and "minority tradition." While her references to women contain no specific markers with respect to race, her choice of Plath and Sexton mark an identification with white women writers. Her references to "dark men" might suggest a Chicana consciousness since "dark men" could include Chicano as well as Black men. However, these references could also suggest her own identification with some white women's preference for Black men as an alternative to their dissatisfaction with white males. Villanueva's poetic feminine consciousness sees itself apart from the dominant male tradition, but it does not particularize itself with respect to the specific non-white group of which she is a member.

With the exception of five poems already published in *Bloodroot,* the rest of the twenty-one pieces in *Poems* were new. These twenty-one poems are dedicated to an elaboration of her identity as a woman. Among the five older pieces are the two poems about her grandmother: "To Jesus Villanueva, with love" and "There were times."[28] From her decision to include these poems, we can infer that she continues to want them to form part of her poetic identity. However, the poetic voice of these poems, expressive of a specific Chicana identity, remains unintegrated with that of the new poems that develop her vision as a woman. When viewing the collection as a whole, the two identities remain separate and juxtaposed, rather than integrated and synthesized.

Summary of "Mother, May I?"

Mother, May I?[29] is about forty pages long and consists of three parts. The first part recounts the joys and games of childhood as the protagonist grows up in a working-class neighborhood in San Francisco with a Mexican grandmother and aunt who speak primarily Spanish. The mother, absent for the most part, appears at strategic moments of the girl's life. In the mother's absence, the girl grows up attached to her grandmother, a wise old woman who becomes her mentor and educator. To the protagonist, her *mamacita* is exceptional: a nurturing mother-figure, a warm disciplinarian, a powerful and human presence. The protagonist mentions her father only once: "sometimes I cried for my / father but I didn't know who / *he* was" (p. 8).

At age six or seven, the girl experiences the trauma of rape. She tells no one about the rape, not even her grandmother. A few years pass, and the mother, we infer, decides to formally relinquish her child to an orphanage: "then she / gives me away / to strangers" (p. 16). The mother also commits the grandmother, now old and sick, to a retirement home. Eventually, the girl is placed in a foster home. She confronts death for the first time when she sees her grandmother die. Part one closes with the girl at her grandmother's funeral where she secretly drops one rose into mamacita's tomb.

In part two, the girl escapes from her foster parents and goes to live with her Spanish-speaking aunt. At thirteen, her romance with a young boy results in pregnancy, and "a child blooms / inside me" (p. 22). However, her childhood romance—"boy meets girl; they fall in love; they marry and live happily ever after"—is ruined by the boy's parents who do not allow them to marry. The girl has the child alone.

The pregnancy results in the mother's return: "my mother keeps me." The girl experiences the pain and joy of childbirth. After a few years, she marries her childhood sweetheart after all and has another child. Her husband goes to fight in a war, probably Viet Nam, and upon his return, conflict ensues: "he drinks too much / and / he hurts me sometimes" (p. 25). Difficult years begin for the protagonist as she searches to find meaning to her life. The husband, "crazy," is eventually locked away. Part two ends with the young woman looking for her grandmother's grave site, a scene that marks the poem's turning point because it is at this site that the protagonist finds her identity as person and poet.

While parts one and two develop the woman's personal history in a linear and causative sequence, part three ruptures the narrative line and becomes more metaphoric. It opens with the death of an intimate friend, whose husband the protagonist marries; she then adopts his children and together with her own children retreats to the countryside. The protagonist experiences motherhood in both a biological and a cultural sense: she has children of her own and by adoption. We imagine the protagonist speaking the rest of the poem in the country, presenting her own "myth of creation" and poetically summarizing the key events already narrated. In the epilogue, the three major dramatic characters — mother, grandmother, and granddaughter — speak their thoughts.

Metaphors, Oppositions, and Transformations

The poem makes the act of a woman's birthing its central metaphor for the two other activities that motivate the protagonist in her quest for self-definition: her drive to "birth" herself as a woman and a person, and her drive to create her poem. The creative process, or self-expression, is thus to be understood in three different contexts: (1) the reproductive cycle of coitus, pregnancy, and birth; (2) the psychological development of becoming a person; and (3) the artistic process of making a cultural artifact such as a poem, a film, or a painting. Since the "I" is the means by which the fictional speaker narrates her story/poem, the birthing of her "I," or personhood, is tied to the artistic act of expression.

The central oppositions organizing the metaphors of the protagonist's quest for self-kowledge as a person and a poet are two. The first opposition is between images of "taking-in" and "giving-out." Related to this first opposition, but not perfectly parallel with it, is a second opposition between acts of repression — or "holding-in" — and acts of expression. The first terms of each opposition — "taking-in" and "holding-in" — though similar as actions, have opposite feelings associated with them. The act of "taking-in" is usually positive, referring often to the physical incorporation of an "object" from the outside, by eating it, for example. The act of "holding-in" is always negative. Unlike the act of "taking-in," which involves bringing something "inside" from the outside, "holding in," or repression, refers to something that is already "inside" and unconscious. The second terms of each opposition — "giving-out" and expression — involve actions of expelling, except that "giving-out" operates in a physical context (feces, babies, or words) and expression in a psychological and artistic context. The events and actions embodying these oppositions are interwoven and interlinked throughout the poem. My discussion of the first opposition integrates examples that relate to the second and more fundamental opposition of repression and expression.

Three actions of "taking-in" and "giving-out" taken from three different categories of experience show how these oppositions organize important events in the protagonist's life. The first action of "taking-in" and "giving-out" involves the biological actions of ingestion and expulsion, or the digestive tract (eating, swallowing) and the gastro-intestinal tract (defecating, expelling). These actions occur during the narrator's early infancy, or the anal phase in Freudian terminology.[30] Delighted by her acts of excreting, the fictional narrator as a little girl encounters the taboo parts of her body. The child's creative impulses lead her to imitate the act of birthing by excreting her feces. She likes to swallow corn kernels and her tiny rubber doll because she loves finding these objects in her excrement, and she enjoys bathrooms because this is where she "makes things." In the naive vision of the child, the rhythmic movement of defecation, a pleasurable straining and releasing, is comparable to giving birth. For her, the process of defecation is "like having babies."

The human body's absorption of food and the excretion of waste or feces is not an exact parallel to the birthing of babies and the writing of poems. By formulating an analogy between the birthing of babies and poems, Villanueva fulfills society's expectations because the results of these activities are generally accepted as good and beneficial. Her insistence that the body's defecation of its excrement is analogous to the other two categories, however, represents an inversion of society's norms. Villanueva makes a counter-culture statement with her excretory theory of poetry: her baby is her poetry but so is her feces because it involves the act of release.

The little girl hears grown-ups talking about birthing, " — you have to push it out / hard." In the adults' language, "it" means "a baby," but the child comically confuses "it" with defecating, reinforcing the analogy between defecating and birthing. Her ability to recognize words and confuse their meaning is also an indication that this is the child's anal phase of development.[31]

> I hear them talking sometimes:
> — you have to push it out
> hard. — I do that. I
> like to look at what I
> make. it even smells
> good to me. sometimes
> they're pretty, when you eat
> too fast
> and the corn comes right out.
> it makes it yellow. one
> time my aunt came in and I
> peed and pooped and I
> said — I just made a
> salad — she didn't
> look too happy. so I kept
> it to myself. (p. 7)

Here, the girl rejoices in having "peed and pooped" and verbalizes this joy to her aunt. Her imagination transforms the excrement into a beautiful salad. The verbal communication of her action, however, produces her aunt's unhappy look, a gesture that encourages the girl to withhold if not the action itself, then at least the telling of the action.

Another time she swallows her tiny rubber doll to "have a baby in / my poop." Again the child's imagination transforms her doll into a baby. The grandmother discovers her swallowing her doll and utters a loving warning, with a smile: " — it'll get stuck and grow as big / as you and you won't have any room / left. — So I stopped" (p. 7). The child stops because the grandmother's soft threat makes her fear that she will not be able to fulfill her fantasy to have a baby.

From the poem's onset, then, the child's creative impulses are in conflict with society's rules. Here, the family in the persons of her aunt and grandmother begin to socialize her, to teach her that she must obey rules and laws. The child expresses her anal impulses but she also quickly learns to control them. The woman narrator looking back on this incident tells us: "and then I learned how / to hide"

(p. 8). The deictic *then* tells us that the woman narrator, now speaking in the present moment of the story's telling, realizes that this is the moment in her childhood when she learned to repress, or "hide," that part of her personality that desired to do pleasurable but taboo things. She learned that she could not do and should not express certain impulses.

This first action takes place in the private environment of the home dominated and controlled by two Mexican women. The second action relates to the category of experience of male-female sexuality, and it takes place in the public, social world. The specific incident is the protagonist's rape by an adult male. This event is an aberration of the sexual and reproductive act in which the woman "takes-in" or "eats," so to speak, the male sperm and releases or creates a baby. The child, seven or eight years old, encounters the horror and trauma of male sexual abuse.

The child is playing in the park with her slightly older friend Peggy when they meet a male stranger (not racially determined) who tells them that playing in the park is illegal. One of them, he says, will have to go with him to sign a book. Peggy, who points to the protagonist and says, "she'll go," runs away, leaving the heroine to confront the stranger alone. The stranger "all of a sudden . . . picked / me up and he wouldn't put / me down" (p. 13). In the face of this threat, the girl invents stories about her mother, naively assuming that they will influence the stranger to let her go. She reverts to arguments from play and fantasy as well as from social differences to convince the rapist to let her go.

> —see this dress? my mother
> bought it for me. she
> has lots of money. she'll
> give you money
> if you let me
> go. look! my dress is pretty
> and new! — I'd been showing
> off that day twirling in circles
> pretending
> I was kidnapped from a king
> and queen
> pretending
> I was rich
> because my dress was so beautiful. (pp. 13-14)

Though her family is lower-class, the girl has assimilated the notion that sordid incidents like the one she is about to experience do not befall people with money. Her references to fantasy, status, and riches are of no avail. The man invites her to "suck something / good," an invitation that constitutes an order because of the context of the situation.

> he put me down.
> he took off my dress.
> he took off my t-shirt.
> he took off my panties.
> and then he said
> — do you want to suck something
> good? —
> and I thought it must be bad.
> it must be licorice because
> I hate it because
> he hates me and
> he wants me to eat
> something bad and maybe
> if I eat something bad
> he'll let me go. so I said
> — o.k. —
> he put it in my mouth
> and it didn't taste like anything.
> it hurt my mouth but I
> wouldn't cry and then
> he made me lie down
> and the stickers hurt
> and I was getting all dirty
> and I knew if I cried
> he'd kill me. (p. 14)

Though it is not explicitly stated, we infer that a *real* rape has taken place. I insist on *real* because it is important to see that rape is not a figure of speech meant to stand for some other kind of experience. Sylvia Plath's sense of psychological estrangement led her to create, in "Lady Lazarus" and "Daddy," for example, psychological forms where hierarchical relationships between society and individual, or between father and daughter, become heavily exaggerated. In "Daddy" she sees herself as a Jewish daughter psychologically tormented by a father who she presents as a brutal Nazi oppressor.[32] While a poet like Sylvia Plath felt it necessary to invent elaborate configurations to capture intense psychological torment, Villanueva talks in the above passage in direct, explicit terms of an actual rape.

The rape in Villanueva's poem represents a real gagging. The rapist forces the girl to put her mouth around the phallus. The positive action of swallowing, or "taking-in," in the first example is replaced in this second example by the negative action of gagging, or "holding-in." The action of gagging also functions metaphorically because it represents the repression of the girl's powers of speech to tell about the action. In the first example the child expressed her biological impulses physically and verbally, though she learned later she was not supposed to do this. In this event she is forced to experience the rape and then is intimidated into repressing it. The action of defecating in the first example, or "giving-out," is also replaced here by the negative action of "holding-in."

She promises not to tell and the stranger lets her go.

> and when my aunt saw me she said
> Peggy told her and the police were
> finding me and I told her
> — I always have to do the dirty
> work —
> and I didn't cry.
>
> it was then I decided to become a boy. (p. 15)

The child cannot really communicate to anyone the words "he raped me." The child probably means the words "I always have to do the dirty work" literally. In other words, rape is dirty work and I, not Peggy, had to do it. Her words displace her original impulse to tell about the concrete oppressive act of rape to a more general and ambiguous event ("dirty work"). In this way she strikes a compromise between telling and not telling: she is able to say what she wants but not in a way that really expresses what happened to her. She sublimates her femininity into a tomboy identity, having learned that little girls are vulnerable to males who have the physical power to oppress them. She takes on the mask of masculinity and an identity with the oppressor. Ultimately, the protagonist represses the telling of the rape, never saying anything about it to anyone.

The protagonist goes through her tomboy phase, fighting the toughest boy in school, climbing roofs and high buildings, and throwing ash trays at her stepfather when she sees him strangling her mother. Soon, the biological process takes its course with the onset of menstruation. "I bled there [in high roofs] the first time / and knew it was special, but I ignored it" (p. 16). The tomboy phase and the coming of menstruation form a minor opposition that metaphorically varies the pattern of "taking-in" and "giving-out." On the one hand, by assuming a tomboy identity, she represses her feminine characteristics; on the other hand, menstruation and puberty bring on their release.

The third action of "taking-in" and "giving-out" takes place during a second journey to her grandmother's grave site, which parallels an earlier visit during her grandmother's funeral. The second visit is more satisfying because it results in a moment of self-knowledge as a person and an artist. This third action functions in a sexual but non-genital context: it involves the physical body in a figurative way. Before explaining the significance of this second visit and its relation to the previous events, especially to the rape incident, a brief summary of the events that intervene is necessary.

Up to this point in the poem, the mother has been present only intermittently in the child's life. Before the death of the grandmother, the mother abandons the girl to an orphanage and commits her mother, the protagonist's grandmother, to a retirement home. The mother, for reasons unrevealed, is present at the grandmother's death. The grandmother dies in the retirement home, where the girl has visited her several times. "I bring her chilis and onions / and comb her hair / and rub her back" (p. 18). This time, the protagonist arrives with her mother and aunt to see her grandmother, and the nurses tell them she is already dead. The girl refuses to believe them. She runs into her grandmother's room and sees her grandmother sit up, utter in Spanish her last wish: "Alma, *no me quiero morir*," and then die. Whether the grandmother is already dead or actually dies at the moment the granddaughter enters the room depends upon whose interpretation of events we choose to believe — the nurses' or the girl's. More importantly, the girl's interpretation is a complete refutation of society's view.

On seeing her grandmother die, the girl screams a cry of pain that is rendered to us in Spanish in all capitals:

> she sat up
> and said
> —Alma, *no me quiero morir*—
> and then she died.
>   AIIIIIIIIII MAMACITA
> mamacita
> and then I cried (p. 18)

These capitals are textual marks indicating that the girl shouts them in a loud *grito* to express the pain and sorrow she feels at losing the person who nurtured and cared for her as a child. The word *mamacita,* containing the word *mamá,* reverberates to suggest the girl's release of the pain she associates with her mother's absence.

The girl's loud verbal release of pain leads to a nonverbal release as she begins to cry. The grandmother's death marks a very important moment in the heroine's life because she releases repressed feelings. However, she is again forced to repress these feelings because the nurses give her medication to make her stop crying.

> and I couldn't stop crying so
> they made me stop with some medicine
> and I didn't cry again.
> I didn't cry that night.
> or the next day.
> or the funeral day. (p. 18)

Instead, she drops one rose into her grandmother's grave and feels it "squish." Rose and girl are identified as the same since both are "squished." The adult-narrator, thinking back to this moment, says,

> and they thought I was selfish
> and stubborn because
> I dressed up in my new shoes
> and a skirt and a red shirt
> and I didn't cry.
>
> they didn't know the rose
> was me. (p. 19)

The rose is the metaphoric containment of the girl's self that for the time being remains repressed. By wearing new shoes, a skirt, and especially the red shirt, she intentionally fails to fulfill society's social code of dress for a funeral, especially one which takes place in a conservative Mexican setting. She does not say anything, but her dress is a defiant, albeit indirect, display of her repressed self.

The years in between her grandmother's funeral (when she is about ten) and the second visit to the grave (when she is twenty-one) are mixed with joy and pain. She experiences joy with an Anglo boy, intended as a bright spot in an otherwise lost childhood.[33]

> we walk, the
> boy and I.
> we speak, the
> boy and I.
> we laugh, the
> boy and I.
> we kiss, the
> boy and I. (p. 21)

The repetition and parallel syntax give this event a fairy-tale tone. She enjoys sexual gratification: "we love / on rooftops, doorways, parks, alleys." She expresses herself in birthing her first child, a positive experience. Years later, she gives birth to a second child by her lover, now her husband. He is taken to war, "to / their armies, their guns, their prisons, their death." When the husband returns, he is angry and "wants to kill something." The fairy-tale aspect of their romance is lost, recoverable only during moments of sexual love: "but when we make love / we are children again."

The predominant tone of these years, however, is silence, frustration, and anxiety. After her rape experience and her grandmother's death, the girl cultivates even more the dissociation between an inner "unembodied" self and an outer "embodied" self.[34] She conceals the inner self from everyone: "there is / a place / inside / me they / cannot enter. that is / where / I'm hiding" (p. 20). The narrator intimated this division in her personality earlier when, as a child, she learned to conceal pleasurable acts associated with her genitals. Her body, or the "embodied" self, wears the social masks and complies with the wishes and desires of others. Her "unembodied" self maintains itself "pure" and "authentic" from the alienation it feels with its real surroundings. Both selves are part of the heroine's repressed personality: the "inner" self because it is protected from all interpersonal relationships; the "outer" self because it remains an unrecognized part of her complete self.

As a consequence of the violation of the rape and the loss of her grandmother, the girl closes off to everything and everyone. Psychologically, she refuses to "open," to "take-in," her surroundings, the very thing she will have to do to achieve personal release and expression. Instead, she affirms denial, a response which leads her to become an isolated, private person. Her denial is underscored dramatically when she becomes a catatonic person. She closes her orifices, a gesture which moves counter to her earlier gesture of having to open her mouth to ingest the semen: "the years / my mouth would open /.and no words would / speak, / my mouth locked tight / and a loneliness grew / that I couldn't name" (p. 26). Reflecting back, the narrator realizes that not only was she separate from others, from her husband, her children, her environment, but she was also separate from herself:

> I put on my masks, my
> costumes and posed for each
> occasion. I conducted myself
> well, I think, but
> an emptiness
> grew
> that no thing
> could fill. I think
>
> I hungered for myself. (p. 27)

Her inner "I" cannot express itself as long as it remains repressed and latent. What she must ultimately do is encounter her inner "I," confront it, and integrate it with the self she does not like.

This is her state of mind when she returns to search for her grandmother's tombstone. Her husband accompanies her, but besides locating the tomb he plays no part in the spiritual interaction between grandmother and granddaughter. In Villanueva's poetic universe, men are excluded from any dynamic participation in the creation of meaning:

> we look for you, my
> husband and I
> we look for you till
> I'm dizzy. are you
> here, mamacita? are you
> here? he says — here
> it is. — he's found
> you, a '13'
> in the ground. they said
> — Jesus Villanueva
> is '13.' —
> I touch the
> one, the
> three.
> I begin to cry
> and no one stops
> me. I didn't
> know it but
> a seed spilled out
> and my mouth
> ate it. I think
>
> that's when the rose took root. (pp. 27-28)

The woman figuratively "swallows" her grandmother's "seed," a sign of a maternal source. The seed is linked with both life and death: with death, because it comes out of the tomb, the terminal experience of the life cycle; with life, because it comes out of the earth. The poem's presupposition is that the earth is the archetypal, feminine origin of all life. The grandmother, literally buried in the earth, becomes a kind of maternal womb which provides the heroine with the "seed" of a new life.[35] Linking the grandmother with the earth creates an image of a figurative womb. This part of the poem echoes the dominant theme of *Bloodroot:* the earth as an archetypal mother. The connection between her grandmother and the earth as a primordial form in *Mother, May I?* is more implicit but, nonetheless, operative. It is a kind of "buried text" in the poem.

The woman's "eating" of the seed parallels her action as a little girl of swallowing her tiny doll. More importantly now, her "eating" of the seed parallels and transforms her action of having to encompass the male genitals with her mouth. This ingestion of the seed is positive and reverses the earlier negative action. The seed represents restoration, the phallus, loss. The seed is a metaphor for the nurturing grandmother and a substitute for the phallus, a metonymy for the rapist.

The passage below immediately follows the one just cited:

> when she left this man she thought
> she'd die.
> but she didn't. she thought
> the sun would go out
> but it didn't.
> and she heard a voice, distant
> and small, but
> she heard it.
> and her mouth opened slightly
> and a word spilled out. the word
>
> was 'I'. (p. 28)

The narrative strategy of the above passage foregrounds the heroine's transformation from nonperson to person. The narration involves an implicit "I" who speaks of herself as a "she" in order to dramatize her birth as an I-subject. This strategy reverses the one of an earlier passage that dramatizes the narrator's divided self.

> *Dreaming*
> the danger of flying
> is coming back. you must
> close your eyes. one
> time I didn't and I saw me
> laying there and I didn't like me
> and I didn't want to come
> back. I thought she
> was disgusting. she
> had to eat and everything. she
> Was stuck. I
> wasn't. I came
> back anyway and then she
> stood up and looked in the mirror
> and scared me
> to life.
>   . . .
> but I kept dreaming, no matter
> how stubborn
> *she* was. (p. 10)

The narrator objectifies herself as "other." The "secret" self she created and desired to be stands outside and looks at her "false" self who she is and hates. Since the mother abandoned her as a child, it makes sense to assume that the child turns inward toward herself the feelings she perceives to be her mother's: "she hates me" becomes "I hate me." Seeing herself only reinforces the self rejected by the mother. The process of "dreaming" enacted in this passage is a way of exorcising in herself a mother's hatred.

As the narrator meditates in present time on a past moment, she reflects an awareness of her divided self. The "I" is the imaginary "authentic" self while the "me" and the "she" are the real "false" selves. The linguistic shifting emphasizes the lack of a secure place that results from her lost identity with her mother. This passage on dreaming enacts the separation of the self in temporal (past-present) and spatial (here-there) dimensions. The narrator identifies with an "I" to dramatize separation and division. In the magical birth passage, the narrator speaks of herself as a "she" in order to dramatize cohesion and union.

The magical birth scene and the graveyard scene together reverse and transform the event with the rapist in the park, completing the protagonist's transformation from nonperson to person. In the rape scene, the process of "taking-in" and expelling was incomplete: the girl "took-in" but did not release. With the magical birth scene, the process of "taking-in" and expelling is complete, since the girl "takes-in" and expels the seed in the form of the word which "spills" out. The woman encounters her "I" as a woman and, in an implicit way, as a Chicana because in returning to her grandmother she is affirming a Mexican identity. The grandmother represents Mexican culture in the poem, a detail to which we will return.

The pattern of swallowing and ejecting the maternal seed suggests the pattern in a woman's reproductive act when she "swallows" the male sperm and eventually expels the child. It is also a metaphor for the artistic process as creation. The seed which the heroine figuratively swallows and ejects is magically transformed into a "word." The grandmother's seed gives the woman the power of speech, the power to birth (to express) her "I," her self. The word "I" is foregrounded in the scoring of the text because it is placed within quotation marks. As such, it suggests a consciousness of the word as word, the basic raw material of a poet and writer. The woman's "I" is both the subject and the device of the poem, the means by which she narrates her story.

In contrast to the satiric representation in "Of utterances" of the

white male artist figuratively copulating with his white muse, Villanueva dramatically rejects this genital model here in favor of a
magical and nongenital one. The seed is absorbed by the mouth,
transformed, and ejected as a *word* by the mouth. The interraction is
between woman and woman, grandmother and granddaughter. This
implicit rejection of genital sexuality is also an implicit rejection of the
protagonist's mother's dependence upon male attention: "she was
always going away with one of *them* [men]. / she was always beautiful
for *them*" (p. 8). We can further add that this moment of self-
knowledge is connected with the woman's decision to leave her
husband, as if to say that she is now able to confront her life alone
rather than remain in an unhappy marriage.

The language attributes an androgynous quality to the grandmother. Her name is Jesús, which in Mexican culture may function
either for a man or a woman, in the latter case as a shortened form of
María de Jesús. The ambiguity of gender in the name Jesús suggests
an attempt to achieve a birth outside a limited sexuality of male-
female relationships. As a name with divine reverberations in
Catholic mythology, Jesús also suggests a nongenital birth since
Christ was conceived within a woman without the aid of a human
male agency. Since the protagonist's grandmother is named Jesús and
since she is the source of her "birthing" as a woman and as a poet, the
divine associations serve to reinforce and underscore the nongenital
aspects of her birth.

Part two ends with a turning inward toward the "I." Repeating the
phrase "I am here" several times to affirm the presence of her "I," the
narrator qualifies it each time. Even the word "simply," which negates
qualification, is attached as a qualifier.

> *inside*
>
> I am here. (do
> you hear me?) hear
> me. hear me.
> I am here. birthing
> (yourself) is
> no easy task.
> I am here. (pleading)
> I am here. (teasing)
> I am here. (taunting)
> I am here. (simply)
> I am here. (p. 29)

Part three abandons the poem's narrative line and urban
landscape and shifts to a more "poetic" style and country landscape.
The actual location of the narrator/character becomes ambiguous.

We never really know where she is, in contrast to the specific and clear locations given in the first two parts: the home, the school, the grave site. For the remainder of the poem, then, we imagine her speaking from the country, the place where she comes to terms with her internal contradictions. By placing the poet in the country, Villanueva employs the convention which portrays the country as a pastoral land, an idealized utopia, removed from the temporal and spatial contingencies characteristic of the city.

The recognition scene between the two selves is dramatized in the passage entitled "*Her myth* (of creation)" (pp. 31-32), where Villanueva makes self-conscious use of an underlying mythical sequence of the quest, the plunge into the unconscious, and rebirth. Descending "alone," anxious, and terrified into a nether world, she sees "dark figures / with bleeding bodies / and staring eyes / with voiceless mouths." She confronts these "demons" when she realizes "they / were me." The symbolic ritual is a figurative representation of the woman's confrontation with her "false" self whose acceptance earlier had threatened pain and hurt. The birthing has released her inner "I" that now looks at the very things she has refused to confront: the self rejected by the mother, the "dead figures," the "they," the enemy, which are at once foreign and familiar, distant and close.[36] She has felt their presence throughout her life but has avoided them by objectifying them as "other." When she realizes the "dead" are really images of herself, she achieves a moment of ecstasy and transcendence (the blinding light, the highest mountain). Realizing that she is not separate from her experiences, that indeed she *is* her experiences, she accepts her life, ugly as some of it may be.

> *Her myth* (of creation)
> it was dark, so dark
> I was lost. so I
> lay down flat
> in my fear
> and dark figures
> with bleeding bodies
> and staring eyes
> with voiceless mouths
> came to me
> and I lay flat
> with fear
> till I realized they
> were me. the dead.
> and when I realized this,
> a light burst through
> the roof (I thought

> I was on the highest
> mountain on earth
> looking, looking
> with a shift
> of my eyes) and the light
> blinded me, so
> I closed them. then I really
> saw and
>
> I was no longer afraid.
> I did not weep.
> I did not laugh.
> I was not old.
> I was not young.
>
> "I am here."
>
> I said. (pp. 31-32)

Specifically, Villanueva's mythic ritual echoes the feminine archetype of the Demeter-Kore story of a violent separation and reunion
between a mother (Demeter) and daughter (Kore or Persephone).
Villanueva forms part of a group of women poets who, preoccupied
with female-female relationships, have employed the Demeter-Kore
myth as an aid in recovering a lost community of mothers, daughters,
and sisters. Alicia Ostriker points out that they use this myth, as well
as others, for altered ends, as Villanueva does here by inverting the
ascents and conquests of male heroism. In Kate Ellis' "Matrilineal
Descent" it is the poet (Demeter) who descends into the dark world to
recover a lost daughter.[37] Villanueva also shares with some modern
women poets their preoccupation with giving birth unaided to themselves, becoming, so to speak, their own mothers and authors of their
poems. With a sense of her own experiences, identity, and voice, the
poet now takes control of her life, giving birth to the girl-child and the
woman-adult who is herself. Since the act of birthing can be read as a
metaphor for female creativity, she births her "I," her poem, her text.
In her own words, "birthing / (yourself) is no easy task."

Social Oppositions

As does much of Chicano prose and poetry, *Mother, May I?*
portrays a dual rather than a multicultural society of different
nationalities and ethnic origins. The social categories that structure
the heroine's society are drawn from the Mexican-Chicano and Anglo
worlds. The central social oppositions have to do with race and
gender.

The racial identity of Villanueva's protagonist does not depend

upon a conflictual relationship between herself as a member of a
social group and the larger society. In fact, she never opposes
dominant society on the basis of race. This protagonist's racial
identity rests on a projection of a nostalgic world of childhood which
she associates with her Mexican grandmother. While the quest in
search of her womanhood and personhood involved a negation of self,
an absorption of the negative and its transcendence, no comparable
process of struggle defines her Chicana self. The Chicana part of the
poetic identity remains fixed in childhood. The feminine part of the
poetic identity challenges the larger society, moving and changing as
it does. The basis of this social conflict is thus gender and not race.

The protagonist remembers her grandmother fondly. The
diminutive *mamacita* connotes endearment, love, and affection. The
opening scene of the poem plays on a light-dark (good-evil; life-death)
contrast, a device used by the poet to set up her readers' expectations
about the characters. The narrating consciousness simulates a child's
mind opening up to the sensitivities of physical light, movement, and
joy. As she tries to make us see what she saw and feel what she felt as a
child, the grandmother is the first person she recalls, associating her
with the light and joys of childhood. Only her grandmother knew her
secret of extracting joys from light.

> I was always fascinated
> with lights then,
> with my hands
> with my fingers
> with my fingertips, because
> if I squinted my eyes at them
> lights sprayed off
> burst off
> and a joy burst inside me
> and it felt good on my
> eyes to see it, so
>
> I squinted my eyes at
> everything in this manner
> and everything had joy
> on it, in it. it was
> my secret. only
>
> my grandma knew. I knew
> she knew by the way
> she looked at things
> long and slow and peaceful
> and her face would shine, lights
> all over, coming out of
> her tiniest wrinkles;

> she became a young girl.
> there were things that could not
> shine lights. we
> avoided these. these things
> took joy. these things
> could make you old. I didn't
> know it then, but
>
> these things were death. (p. 5)

The mamacita, then, and also the aunt who cares for the heroine once the former dies, are coded as positive — nurturant, responsive, and kind. The grandmother is linked with the Spanish language not only because we are told it is her language but also because we are told that she has taught the girl the Spanish she knows. References to the Spanish language relate to the maternal, nurturing aspects of the girl's education. In one incident the girl laughs at her grandmother who frantically searches for the hat that all along sits on her head. The grandmother gently reprimands her for her rudeness.

> and she spat — *grocera!* — and it
> made me laugh harder and she gave
> me the hand that meant a spanking
> (and she never spanked me)
> and she laughed too (pp. 9-10)

The narrator's description of her memories of her grandmother evokes love, warmth, joy, and peace.

> we
> go to movies and chinatown and shopping.
> she holds one side of the shopping bag, I
> hold the other. we
> pray and dunk *pan dulce* in coffee. we
> make tortillas together. we
> laugh and take the buses
> everywhere. when we
> go to the movies she cries and
> she dances when she irons. I
> comb her long hair and rub her
> back with alcohol. (p. 9)

Since the grandmother is described in terms of habits and thoughts that are more typical of a preliterate society than a literate one, we may assume that she comes from a predominantly oral culture. Her modes of thinking and behavior can be described as formulaic, according to Walter Ong's definition of formulary devices that he claims are typical of oral cultures. A formulary device is any standardized verbal expression, such as an epithet, adage, or proverb,[38] and as such forms part of the thought processes and discourses of an oral culture. The grandmother, for example, resorts to patterned expressions and forms of behavior that she has known and practiced all her life and that she probably learned in an oral context from someone else. When her granddaughter expresses herself by going outdoors without panties, she tells her she must wear long pants under her dresses so the wind cannot smell her. The grandmother assumes an empathetic relationship between nature and the body, implying that nature can fertilize the girl if she is not careful. She uses animistic explanations of an oral tradition to persuade the child to modify her behavior. Her explanation of how she knew when her children were dying is another case in point: "they always / pointed up with their fingers." The grandmother has standardized, well-defined meanings and responses for certain events, and she recalls and applies them to the situation when she needs to.

The grandmother's world — preliterate, preconscious, and utopic — forms one pole of the oppositional dyad of race. The antagonist force is the public world and its institutions. The characters connected with the public world are coded as negative — insensitive, impersonal, and hostile. They are the rapist, the white female school teacher who tolerates no Spanish in her classroom, the nun at the Catholic school who slaps the girl's hands with the ruler (pp. 12-13), the nurses, and the doctor who keeps looking at his watch while the protagonist gives birth (p. 24). Although these characters represent the public sphere, which in the context of the poem must be seen as "Anglo," they are presented as defective primarily because they stand for values we have come to associate with traditional "masculine" culture: the repression of spontaneous feeling, the supremacy of "mind" over "matter" or reason over body, technology over nature, the devalued occupation of women as mothers and nurturers.

That the primary impulse propelling the protagonist's conflict with society is sexual and not racial is clear from specific events in the poem such as the rape incident. At other times, the heroine experiences a male world by way of women who behave like female enforcers of male authority. For example, the nurses at the retirement home suppress the flood of tears that overwhelm the girl when her grandmother dies. A release of emotion through tears is permitted to women in most male-oriented cultures whereas men are not permitted the same release. When the nurses give the girl medication to stop her uncontrollable tears, the poem exposes how well the nurses have internalized a male value — that tears are undesirable and a sign of weakness.

We may obtain a clearer picture of the way women function as female enforcers of male values by reflecting upon the characters, actions, and symbols presented in section 5 of the poem.

> the nun asked to look at
> my hands. I thought she thought
> they were beautiful, so I
> put them out
> and she hit them with
> a ruler. it hurt it hurt
> and she told me to
> put them out
> again and I wouldn't and she
> tried to grab my hands so
> I grabbed the ruler and hit
> her and ran
> home and my grandma let me
> stay when she saw
> my hands. there was
> a beautiful young nun who
> sat in the dark on the other
> side of the cage. the metal was black,
> and cold and beautiful. it had flowers
> and I loved to put my face on it, it
> felt so good and cold.
> and when she came and sat and spoke
> her voice was very warm. she
> said she came from mexico. I
> bet she didn't let them shave
> her head. this boy who was
> very bad sat behind me
> and he put his fingers in my *nalgas*
> when we prayed and when I turned
> and stared at him, he'd
> smell them and smile. he
> whispered one time in the yard
> — they all have bald heads. — (pp. 12-13)

This passage offers two opposing versions of a catholic nun: a "bad" nun who functions as an agent of male power, and her antithesis, a "good" nun. When the "bad" nun asks to see her hands, the girl naively supposes that the nun wants to see them because she thinks them beautiful. The child quickly learns her mistake. We perceive this nun as negative because she hits the child's hands with a ruler for no apparent reason. When the girl says, "I / bet she didn't let them shave her head," meaning the "good" nun, we may infer that the "bad" nun is perceived as bald while the "good" nun is perceived with hair on her head. A second inference is that the "bad" nun is an agent of the Catholic Church, the "them" who shave women's heads. The "good" nun has some sense of self-autonomy.

The presupposition about hair, a conventional one, is that hair is a symbol of sexuality. The shaven head is, therefore, the absence of sexuality; it also suggests the repression of sexual thoughts. For its shape and austerity, a bald head may connote phallic associations. This nun is a masculine, phallic-headed nun. The ruler, linked with the nun, is also a phallic sign and gives this "bad" nun a masculine identity. The hand she slaps, when contrasted with the ruler, connotes femininity for its shape and open position in this situation. The nun striking the girl's hands with the ruler, then, is a kind of symbolic rape and foreshadows the real rape immediately to follow in the poem's next section. If we take the ruler for a masculine symbol, then the nun can represent an extension of masculine society, a female enforcer of masculine authority.

The "good" nun is a fusion of two opposing states. Unlike the conventional bald nun, she has hair on her head, and thus she suggests sexuality. Yet, she is a nun, presumably a virgin and a celibate. She has sexual potency because she is a virgin, but as a celibate she has chosen to deny herself genital sexuality with men. We have in the figure of the beautiful young nun a fusion of two codes: a biological, natural code of virginity (a man or woman either has it or does not), and a cultural code of celibacy (a decision made by a woman or man in culture). This harmonious fusion of sexuality and celibacy, reinforced by the notation that this beautiful nun comes from Mexico and speaks both English and Spanish, is what the poem's narrating consciousness desires and strives to attain, something it does in the poem's epilogue.

To obtain her desired dream vision, the daughter must reconcile herself with her mother. Though this reconciliation addresses tensions in the mother-daughter relationship rather than racial attitudes in second and third family generations, the narrator's closing words in the epilogue suggest, nonetheless, a symbolic harmonization of the paradoxes and ambiguities concerning race in the mother's attitudes.

Ethnically, the mother is Mexican but socially and culturally she has assimilated the values of the mainstream. So, while the grandmother's (and the aunt's) identities fit unambiguously into a Mexican world, the mother, in contrast, lies ambiguously between the Anglo and Mexican worlds. In "Legacies and Bastard Roses," a poem in *Bloodroot* echoed explicitly in *Mother, May I?*—and whose relationship to it we will note in the next section—we learn that though her family's advice was to "marry a good Mexican boy," she was more favorably disposed to Anglo men: "the sun on a / gringo's hair makes me / worship / them." When she returns in *Mother, May I?* at the time of her daughter's first pregnancy, she does so claiming, "we women stick together." The tragic irony, of course, is inescapable since her previous action had been to give her daughter away "to strangers." When she accompanies her daughter to the clinic, she defends her daughter's decision to go through the pregnancy alone, but she does so from self-righteous motives. She tells the clinic secretary: "*she* didn't want to marry *him*." The rhetorical emphasis on the two pronouns suggests that the mother knows the boy's family has forbidden the marriage because the girl is Mexican.

> —I [the boy] can't marry you. they [boy's family]
> won't let me. they
> say,
> she'll have 12 more
> kids in 10 years, you
> know those people.
> they say
> NO— (p. 22)

Instead of acknowledging that her daughter has been the victim of racial discrimination, she denies it, entertaining the fantasy that her Mexican daughter rejected the Anglo boy. The mother believes "Anglo" is better than "Mexican." Her aspirations, after all, were to "marry Anglo."

In the epilogue, the poet presents her utopian vision of the merger between "woman" and "Chicana." Neither the grandmother nor the aunt can function as models for the protagonist. Though she admires these women, she cannot fulfill herself in the same way they did. Theirs is a world gone by, whose circumstances limited women of their social class to the domestic sphere. However, her mother—the more public, active woman—offers her no real fulfilling model either. So while her poetic "I" includes an awareness of both first and second generation women in her family, it also represents a transformation of each. She affirms the contribution that each has made to the formation of her personal identity.

> *Epilogue*
> as in all
> stories, there is a
> story within a
> story. there is the
> story of my friend (the

one who walked
with me to the
hospital; she was why
I beat up the
toughest boy in school,
because he was going
to beat her up; she was my
best friend since 12; she still
is) who somehow
is always
there. her soft
eyes always
recognize
me.

(mom)

men come
and go. your friends

stay. women
stay. mom
said. perhaps

this is a story of
women raging against
women; of
women loving
women; of
women listening to
women, because
men don't have time
to because
men move
on, because
men haven't learned
how to
listen, to
speak as
women; so

the thread, the story
connects
between women;
grandmothers, mothers, daughters,
the women
the thread of this
story.

(mamacita)

when a man opens a woman, she
is like a rose, she
will never close
again.

ever.

(me)
pistils. stamens.
wavering in the sun.
a bloom on the bush.
a mixed bloom.
they wonder at it.
a bastard rose.
a wild rose.
colors gone mad.
a rupture of thorns.
you must not pluck it.
you must recognize
   a magic rose
          when
you see it.

                (excerpted from my poem
                Legacies and Bastard Roses)
                (pp. 37-39)

The mother appears transformed within a network of continuity and relationship with other women. She has learned that only women can provide other women with friendship.

(mom)
men come and go. your friends
stay. women
stay. mom
said. (p. 38)

The order of presentation of the speakers is not the generational sequence of grandmother, mother, granddaughter, but rather mother, grandmother, and granddaughter. The placement of the speakers suggests that the poet feels closer to her grandmother than to her mother. This placement reinforces the grandmother's role as a mediating agent because she nurtured the girl in the absence of her real mother. She also acted as a mediating agent in a metaphoric way at the magical grave scene where she offered the heroine a way to move from a negative to a positive life. Mamacita's text is the original source out of which her own text emerges.

By juxtaposing her own passage with mamacita's, however, she makes us see the difference between them. She tells us that she is a "rose" just like her mamacita said, but when she says "rose" she means it in a different sense than her mamacita did.

(mamacita)
when a man opens a woman, she
is like a rose, she
will never close
again.

ever. (p. 39)

The grandmother's philosophy upholds a traditional view that virginity in a woman is desirable. Her words communicate a nostalgia for the loss of the ideal "closed" rose in her system of values. They also posit a reliance on an outside male agent to initiate a woman's growth and development: a man "opens" a woman.

In the closing fragment expressing her own identity, the metaphor of the rose reverberates to include her grandmother's rose, but while her grandmother's rose, once opened, would never close again, the poet's rose is a sign of her rebirth. She is "pistils. stamens. / wavering in the sun." Alone, content, and self-sufficient, her maturation does not depend upon any outside agency. She is a "wild rose." An "open" rose means power, wisdom, and beauty in Villanueva's poetic scheme. The poet hears her grandmother's statement about the traditional rose in a way no one else does.

(me)

pistils. stamens.
wavering in the sun.
a bloom on the bush.
a mixed bloom.
they wonder at it.
a bastard rose.
a wild rose.
colors gone mad.
a rupture of thorns.
you must not pluck it.
you must recognize
a magic rose
when
you see it.

(excerpted from my poem
Legacies and Bastard Roses)
(p. 39)

The poet's fragment also recuperates other images used in the autobiography. The image of the sun, for example, recalls the mother who in "Legacies and Bastard Roses" worshipped the "sun on a gringo's head." In part two of *Mother, May I?*, the poet referred to her first husband, who was Anglo, as her "sun": "he is my sun. I / turn and turn toward / him" (p. 25). When she decided to leave him, "she thought, the sun would go out / but it didn't." In the poet's text, the image of the sun does not suggest female dependence upon men, as it does in the other two contexts. Instead, the language flaunts the speaker's independence from a social world of real men and women. The poet celebrates the feminine and masculine aspects of herself ("pistils. stamens") within a context of a mythical, magical world. The parallel placement of the word "pistils" and "stamens" on the same line suggests equality and harmony rather than the sexual asymmetry that characterizes woman's experiences in the social world.

The images also reverberate in a racial context. The images of "a mixed bloom," "a bastard rose," and "a wild rose" suggest the botanical phenomenon of hybridization — a mixing of strains. We can extrapolate the images from a botanical to a social context, where hybridization suggests racial mixtures, a form of *mestizaje*. Race is "colors gone mad." The poet is giving positive meaning to something that is considered negative in most cultures: *bastard*. Literally, she is a "bastard" child because she never knew who her father was. The idea of "bastard" also connects with the Chicano experience in the sense that in U.S. culture "Chicano" is an "unlegitimated" presence. Thus unlike her mother, who perhaps never could, the poet affirms her Mexican-Chicano self in a positive way.

Villanueva displays herself as the unusual rose she perceives herself to be. Within the events of the poem, the protagonist flaunts her person at her grandmother's funeral by wearing new shoes, a skirt, and a red shirt. Here, her gesture involves the performance of a language event: she speaks metaphorically. By doing so, she arrives at a statement of personal self-definition that harmonizes feminine with masculine, Chicano with Anglo. Symbolically, she fuses race and sex.

UNIVERSITY OF CALIFORNIA, SAN DIEGO

Notes

[1](Pittsburgh, Pennsylvania: Motheroot Publications, 1978).

[2](Austin, Texas: Place of Herons Press, 1977).

[3]In *Third Chicano Literary Prize* (Irvine, California, 1976-77), pp. 85-133.

[4]James Cody, Villanueva's editor of *Bloodroot*, explains his fascination with her

poems with reasons that distort the issue of why Villanueva writes in the first place. In his introductory comments, Cody, in so many words, claims he liked Villanueva's poetry because she writes like a man: "her poems were of the universal quality, embracing all subjects and passions, that seemed . . . to come almost only from the writings of men. In addition, there was none of the self-pity that is in so much 'feminist' poetry." He goes on, "she does not ape men or brutalize her sexuality to escape the bonds that have existed traditionally for women. For her these bonds do not exist. Alma Villanueva is not a feminist, or a female poet, she is a poet" (p. i).

⁵In a conversation with Alma Villanueva on May 24, 1983, she said she had not read Walt Whitman prior to writing *Bloodroot*. While confirming this in his introduction to *Bloodroot*, James Cody insists on the resemblance of Villanueva's poems to Whitman: "Though Alma had read almost no Whitman before our friendship began, I read her poems as if she were the female fulfillment of those words spoken so long ago" [by Whitman in "Poets to Come"]. Cody saw "a clarity of line, a forthrightness, a subconscious and assumed rhythm . . . that seemed to proceed from Whitman" and ". . . that insouciant joy in the crude, the ordinary, the common, while elevating it, or accepting it equally with the rest of life" (p. ii). Had Villanueva read Whitman prior to writing *Bloodroot*, I suspect that an unconventional poet like Whitman who allowed practically everything to enter into his poems, employed free verse, used no rhyme, and believed in spontaneous natural song, would have interested and appealed to Villanueva.

⁶See Fernando Alegría's *Walt Whitman en Hispanoamérica* (Mexico: Ediciones Studium, 1954), especially pp. 314-31.

⁷Referring to *Song of Myself* and Neruda's "Ritual de mis piernas," Alegría points to this difference in the way each poet speaks about his legs. See pp. 320-31.

⁸See "Cuerpo de mujer," the introductory poem in *Veinte poemas de amor y una canción desesperada* (p. 87), and poems II, V, VI, and XIII (pp. 87-91 and 95-96) in *Obras Completas*, 3rd ed. (Buenos Aires: Editorial Losada, 1967), I, 87-106. For an English version see *Twenty Love Poems and a Song of Despair*, trans. W. S. Merwin, bilingual ed. (London: Jonathan Cape, 1969).

⁹For a general overview and orientation to Plath's and Sexton's poetry and an understanding of their place in contemporary American poetry, see Gary Lane's *Sylvia Plath: New Views on the Poetry* (Baltimore: Johns Hopkins University Press, 1979); Charles Newman's *The Art of Sylvia Plath: A Symposium* (Bloomington: Indiana University Press, 1970); Mary Lynn Broe's *Protean Poetic* (Columbia: University of Missouri Press, 1980); and Karl Malkoff's *Crowell's Handbook of Contemporary American Poetry* (New York: Thomas Y. Crowell, 1973).

¹⁰Alicia Ostriker, "The Thieves of Language: Women Poets and Revisionist Mythmaking," *Signs*, Vol. 8, No. 1 (Autumn 1982), pp. 68-90. Ostriker observes that childish language and the bawdy are variants of colloquial language. She notes that Rachel Blau Du Plessis uses "punning baby talk" in her poem "Medussa" to reveal "the power of sexual pain to thwart growth," while in Sexton it signals sexual trauma. She asserts that Erica Jong is one poet who uses the bawdy to invade the linguistic preserves of male discourse, pp. 87-88.

¹¹Barbara Hernstein Smith, *Poetic Closure: A Study of How Poems End* (Chicago: The University of Chicago Press, 1968), p. 15. For a more extensive analysis of the poetic identity, see my book, *Contemporary Chicana Poetry: A Critical Approach to an Emerging Literature* (University of California Press, 1985). In my book I argue that *Mother, May I?* must ultimately be considered as the author's actual written utterance to a specific

audience. In light of this analysis, Villanueva's two identities of woman and Chicana remain separated rather than joined.

[12]In *Bloodroot*, pp. 4-5.

[13]I cite these lines exactly as they appear. At times, Villanueva closes a parenthesis without ever having opened it.

[14]In *Bloodroot*, p. 1. The lines cited are the entire poem.

[15]In *Bloodroot*, pp. 2-3, "(wo)man," "bloodroot," and "ZINZ" offer a good example of a feminine analogue to the myth of Aztlán in Chicano poetry in the late 1960s and early 1970s. According to this myth, Aztlán, reputedly in today's Southwest, was the legendary birthplace of the Aztec Indians. The Aztlán myth posits the existence of a collective unconscious for modern-day Chicanos whereby they retain continuity with their Indian heritage. For some Chicanos, Aztlán makes possible a reintegration with their cultural roots. The Aztlán myth represents a unilateral rejection of national U.S. culture.

Villanueva does something similar in a feminine context. While Aztlán is a mythical utopia based on race, Villanueva's mythical matriarchy is based on gender. Like the poets of Aztlán (one example is the early Alurista of the *Floricanto* poems, 1971), Villanueva, too, criticizes Western culture: men have split the world into mind and body. Her revision is to affirm and celebrate the beauty of the feminine body, which constitutes the pole of the opposition negated by Western civilization and, therefore, the aspect of the human person to be elevated. Alejandro Morales has discussed this feminine principle in terms of Mircea Eliade's Earth Mother in "Terra Mater and the Emergence of Myth in *Poems* by Alma Villanueva," *Bilingual Review, 7*, no. 2 (1980), pp. 123-42.

[16]In *Bloodroot*, pp. 21-22.

[17]Roy Harvey Pearce, *Whitman* (New Jersey: Prentice Hall, 1962), p. 6.

[18]Villanueva uses no apostrophe to indicate the possessive.

[19]In *Bloodroot*, p. 37. I cite the entire poem. This poem bears a thematic resemblance to Neruda's "Unidad," the fifth poem in *Residencia en la tierra I (1925-31)*. The concern for the poet's immediate sensory experience, the eternal repetition of natural events (the ebb and flow of the sea), and the subject's experience of time as "intuited pastness" are some common themes. See Lane Kauffmann, "Neruda's Last Residence: Translations and notes on four poems," *The New Scholar*, Vol, 5, No. 1 (1975), pp. 122-24.

[20]In *Bloodroot*, pp. 49-51.

[21]In *Bloodroot*, pp. 57-59.

[22]In *Bloodroot*, pp. 52-54.

[23]In *Bloodroot*, p. 54.

[24]Indications of a witch-persona in Plath are mentioned by Gary Lane on pp. 13 and 144. Ostriker observes that the framing element of Sexton's *Transformations* is the persona of the narrator-poet, "a middle-aged witch, me," p. 86.

[25]In *Poems,* pp. 117-18.

[26]In *Poems*, "Of/to Man," p. 115; "witches' blood," p. 105; and "Of utterances," pp. 107-08. In the publication of *Poems,* "witches' blood" mistakenly appears as part of the poem "The Hard Probing Plow." The poem begins with the words "witches' blood" on p. 105 and concludes with the same on p. 106.

[27]A proponent of this theory of poetry was Robert Graves who, in *The White Goddess* (New York: Vintage Books, 1960), originally published in 1948, argued that a test of a poet's vision is the "accuracy of his portrayal of the White Goddess and of the island over which she rules," and "a true poem is necessarily an invocation of the White

Goddess, or Muse, the Mother of All Living" (p. 12). For Graves, poetry is a "magical" language that honored the Moon Goddess in prepatriarchal times, survived in popular religious ceremonies and mystery cults, and was still taught during the times of the early Christian Emperors "in the poetic colleges of Ireland and Wales, and in the witch-covens of Western Europe." He argues that one important difference between the classical and Romantic poet was his attitude toward the "White goddess." While the classical poet claimed to be the Goddess's master, the Romantic poet of the nineteenth century was a "true poet only in his fatalistic regard for the Goddess as the mistress who commanded his destiny," pp. 12-13.

In the same conversation of March 24, 1983, Villanueva asserted that she did not quote Graves in this poem but rather Sexton's quotation of Graves on the "White Goddess." As with Neruda and Whitman, Villanueva seems to have come across a source in an indirect way, in this case Graves via Sexton, since she claims she had not read Graves at the moment of writing this poem.

28In *Bloodroot*, pp. 52-56.

29Numbers in parentheses refer to the pages of this poem where the cited passages appear.

30Norman Holland, *The Dynamics of Literary Response* (New York: Oxford University Press, 1968), pp. 38-39. Holland's explanation of the phases of child development within a psychoanalytical context are helpful for understanding the character's activities as a little girl. See pp. 32-50.

31*Ibid.*, p. 39.

32For some comments on Plath's exaggerated hyperboles, see Richard Allen Blessing, "The Shape of the Psyche: Vision and Technique in the Late Poems of Sylvia Plath," and Marjorie Perloff, "Sylvia Plath's 'Sivvy' Poems: A Portrait of the Poet as Daughter," in Gary Lane's *Sylvia Plath,* esp. pp. 66-67 and p. 173.

33Villanueva's male characters fall into categories of sexual deviants or innocent wimps. The rapist and the uncle who molests the child (see pp.6-7 and 13-15) are examples of the former, and the Anglo schoolboy the protagonist falls in love with is an example of the latter. The only male character in the poem with whom the protagonist seems to have a positive relationsip is the second husband, but about him we know nothing. Men do not play any significant role in Villanueva's poetic universe, since they do not participate in the creation of meaning. This is also true of sons, who the narrator dismisses with a passing reference before moving into her discusion of the mother-daughter bond (see pp.34-35).

In her article "On Female Identity and Writing by Women," Judith Kegan Gardiner points out that Anglo women writers depict their male characters around the notion of access to power: "they are wimps or brutes." *Critical Inquiry* (Winter 1981), p. 356. Villanueva seems to share this tendency with Anglo women writers because her male characters are so one-dimensional. This, of course, is in keeping with her primary objective of telling a woman's story. Within the context of Chicano literature written by males, men have primarily offered limited portrayals of women in roles as either virgins or whores. Villanueva's portrayal of men is a neat reversal of this process.

34These terms are R. D. Laing's in *The Divided Self* (Baltimore: Penguin Books, 1965), pp. 65-77.

35In "Terra Mater and Emergence of Myth" (see note 15), Alejandro Morales follows Mircea Eliade's discussion of myth and focuses on the archetype of the earth mother and its function in the figure of the grandmother in Villanueva's prize-winning anthology *Poems*. Morales sees the grandmother as the contemporary incarnate form of the archetype Terra Mater. Unlike Morales, I am not interested in validating the Eliade model of myth, but I do think that Villanueva consciously knows and uses archetypal conventions. She says in Elizabeth Ordóñez' study of her life and work (*Chicano Literature: A Reader's Encyclopedia,* ed. Julio A. Martínez [Westport, CT: Greenwood Press, forthcoming]) that she has been influenced by Mary Esther Harding's *Woman's Mysteries: Ancient and Modern* (New York: G. P. Putnam's Sons, 1971). Harding is an archetypalist, a disciple of Jung, who introduced her book originally published in 1935. One of Harding's objectives in *Woman's Mysteries* is to expose and recover the "feminine principle" repressed by Western culture via the presentation of feminine archetypes such as the Demeter-Kore myth. The intention of making the grandmother in the grave scene a kind of "earth mother" is a buried presupposition of the poem.

[36]Freud's definition of the repressed. See "The Uncanny," tr. Alix Strachey, in *Sigmund Freud On Creativity and the Unconscious* (New York: Harper Torchbooks, 1958), p. 148.

[37]Ostriker, esp. pp. 72-75.

[38]Walter J. Ong, "Literate Orality of Popular Culture," in *Rhetoric, Romance, and Technology* (Ithaca & London: Cornell University Press, 1979), p. 289. Also appropriate on formulary devices and their relation to oral cultures are Ong's comments in "Transformations of the Word and Alienation," in *Interfaces of the Word* (Ithaca and London: Cornell University Press, 1977), pp. 17-22.